René Johnson

Leaving Your
Comfort Zone

HOW TO LEAD
YOUR LIFE FROM
THE POWER
ZONE!

Copyright © 2009

Leaving Your Comfort Zone:
How to Lead Your Life From The Power Zone!

By René Johnson

Publisher: Emerggy Coaching, LLC www.emerggy.com
Portions from ebook, Leaving The Comfort Zone © 2006

This book may be purchased in bulk for educational, business, fundraising, or sales promotional use. For information, please contact us at www.powerzonecoach.com

Editors: Nye Thuesen and Ruth Campbell
Cover design and graphics: Joshua Luchau, www.ctrlpdesign.com

ISBN 13: 9780615307169

Printed in the United States of America

V20

Acknowledgements

To my clients who have allowed me to serve you on your journey to success —Thank you for allowing me to "Show Up"!

To my dear supporters: Annette, Asbury, Jane, Josh, Leslie, Nye, Pat, Paula, Ruthie, Tammy — Thank you for believing in my vision and cheering me on!

Table of Contents

Chapter Five
Principle #5 Understanding the Qualities of a Confident Woman

Chapter Six
Principle #6 Become an Empowered Leader

I could feel my personal greatness, something we all possess, and I could feel my core driving energy beckoning me to explore who I could become and even who I already was. I just needed the vehicle to deliver it.

Preface

This book has been three years in the making. With so much I wanted to share, my biggest challenge was filtering through to the nuggets of what benefits my clients the most and what I have successfully implemented, so that I could encapsulate them into a step-by-step guide to allow you, as the reader, to get the most out of it.

As a coach, I've wanted to make sure you would have the opportunity to create personal awareness and utilize methods and suggestions to turn that awareness into powerful shifts and actions to begin your transformation. Right from the beginning, I desire to help you connect with your own personal power and step into your journey to success.

Here's a little about my own journey to success. Since I was a little girl I've felt a sense of purpose and had a message bigger than myself that I wanted to impart to others. My message was always fueled by a sense of a calling and passion to find it, but not from feeling I was better than anyone. I just knew I had something I was supposed to do. I could feel my personal greatness, something we all possess, and I could feel my core driving energy beckoning me to explore who I could become and even who I already was. I just needed the vehicle to deliver it.

I tried on different roles, trying to find the right fit. Parts would connect but I didn't feel as whole or as powerful as I could be. In my journey to find my personal power, I made mistakes and didn't always have the skills to see the opportunities in my challenges. I had to learn how to quit making judgments that would hold me back and instead accept, forgive, and let go. When I learned this, it allowed me to enjoy more of the discovery process and eventually relax into my gifts and talents so I could stop fighting them.

When I discovered coaching, it felt so natural it was like putting on a perfectly fitted glove and stepping into my complete self. My training provided me with the knowledge and tools to enhance my gifts, which allowed my confidence to increase, and helped me claim my purpose: to serve you. It was such an energizing, liberating, and empowering experience that it was like coming home.

My life path has been filled with courage, unrelenting spirit, and many defining moments to reach the point where I am today. My spirit desires to serve, teach, and inspire women like you to step into their own personal greatness. I firmly believe women can be bigger than any challenge or circumstance they may face.

At some point, each of us will face our own destiny and the choice to grow beyond where we are now in order to fulfill our main purpose in this life. I firmly believe it will involve some form of sharing with others. That's the lifeblood of the cycle of life. I know it is a gift to have found mine and to have the good fortune to use it for good to serve strong women like you.

I am honored you have found your way to this book. I am also thrilled to challenge you to explore the boundaries of your comfort zone and to embrace the personal greatness that awaits you in your Power Zone.

Even with all my desires and hopes for you, I realize I cannot change you. You hold the key to your success. It rests on how much you are willing to believe in yourself in spite of dealing with everyday obstacles or other adversities you may face. It also depends on how much desire you have to stay true to your goals and your ability to stay in tune with the power in you. The challenge, or rather, the opportunity, is about understanding how to tap into your personal power and show up as your true, higher self, 100 percent of the time.

I realize this can be difficult to do. But as women working to attain your goals and dreams, especially considering all you have to deal with on a daily basis at work and in your life, I feel strongly it is important now more than ever that you understand how to tap into your personal power zone. This will help you stay on course toward your journey to success. It will have a direct impact not only on your ability to achieve your personal vision of success but also on those you lead and influence.

One of my favorite quotes sits in a frame on my desk, as it has for many years now, so it stays in the forefront of my thoughts:

> *"Nothing great has ever been achieved except by those who dared believe something inside of them was superior to circumstances."* —Bruce Barton

This has been an inspiring reminder that I CAN achieve great things if only I dare to believe I am greater than any circumstance or doubt I may face. I am passionate about what I do. This passion has been fueled by my clients' success and the powerful results they've received, all from applying the principles I will share with you. It also comes from having to practice what I preach as I have experienced doubt and felt the pain of getting off course and working harder than I needed to, only to come back to honoring this process, and tapping into my power zone, where things become easier and much more enjoyable!

It is important that you know I understand what it is like being a professional, passionate, and goal-driven woman, as I want to collaborate with you in the process you are about to embark upon. Through the years, I have had to leave my comfort zone and take essential risks, both personally and professionally, to get where I am today. Because of my earlier experiences, I soon found that I became more aware of when others were holding themselves back. I could see the greatness that they couldn't see. I naturally became a cheerleader and a coach.

As I paid attention and took notes, I started incorporating some principles I discovered into my work even before my coaching education. In doing so, I recognized four recurring universal truths:

- The human spirit wants to succeed above all else.

- The human capacity to do so is greater than we realize.

- The human tendency to fear change can bring up some strong limiting beliefs, making it difficult to fulfill our true greatness.

- Lastly, we are creatures of habit, and though we may know better or even desire more, we don't always do what's best for ourselves.

I believe that if you trust in the possibilities, and most importantly, in yourself, you can achieve great things. That belief, coupled with a clear vision of success, will show you the way to move forward. The support and teachers you need will show up, and the opportunities to fulfill your vision will be there — if you are open to receive them and are willing to do the work.

If you have ever felt possibilities stirring up inside you but have been unable to see them through, this book will provide a structure to recapture and implement them.

If you wish you could do things differently whether in your personal goals, in a corporate culture, or in the confines of your own business, this book will enable you to identify your blockers and discover the tools to challenge them.

If looking at the description of this book brings up feelings of guilt for things you feel you should have done — the unfulfilled possibilities in your life — don't worry, you are in the right place.

Your challenge right from the beginning will be to shift that guilt into desire. Your journey to this point has not been for naught; rather, now you can stand on the shoulders of your experiences, knowledge, successes, and even your failures to propel yourself toward your next level of achievement.

I'm confident that you CAN turn your possibilities into reality if you are willing to change your thinking and take bold new steps.

Through the **Six Power Zone Principles**™, you'll learn how to create an exciting vision and design the legacy you want to leave behind. You'll identify where you can benefit from changing your thinking and behaviors so you can let go of limiting beliefs and summon the power that already exists in you. You'll discover where to put your focus and how to create strategic steps that will propel you forward and enable you to sustain your gains. You'll face and conquer your confidence blockers then use your newfound confidence to find your voice and value, inspire changes, and lead those changes to the finish line, once and for all.

I truly hope to inspire you to connect with the power in you by providing the method to "Leave Your Comfort Zone" so you can achieve your biggest, most rewarding goals with greater ease and confidence, and take charge by becoming a "driver" rather than a "passenger" in your life. You CAN discover unlimited possibilities that await you in the power zone.

Here's to the power in you!

René Johnson

The Power Zone Coach

Everything you want lies just outside of your comfort zone. You deserve more, so accept the challenge and welcome the changes ahead.

Introduction

The Power Zone

"I was always looking outside myself for strength and confidence but it comes from within; it is there all the time."   *—Anna Freud*

What is the Power Zone?

---

*Recognizing and tapping into our personal power zone is an
essential life skill, one that will help you become a passionately
empowered leader in all areas of your life.*

The Power Zone is a fitting description of an amazing place
inside all of us that holds our personal greatness and core
driving energy. This is our higher place of self-awareness,
personal truth, and power. All success comes from this
place!

When you are in touch with your power zone enough to lead
your life from it, you can focus your energy on anything you
wish to achieve and work clearly and with intention. Ideas
flow easily, confidence and energy are on fire, and you
embrace your personal greatness with excitement and
passion. As a result, you feel inspired to produce significant
transformations in all areas of your life!

I have been inspired and influenced by others who I believe
have found their power zones and are living their lives from
them. I know this because they are making a difference in
the lives of others and in the world around them.

One such person I admire for doing this is Dr. Wayne W.
Dyer. Through his works, I have further defined my
greatness and inspired myself to manifest it. In fact, from
reading his books, I kept myself inspired during the course
of writing this book, and felt empowered by the influence of
his words. I, too, desire to be able to positively influence and
inspire others with my words to manifest their own
greatness.

**When you are working from inspiration, you know you
are working from your power zone!**

Dr. Wayne W. Dyer, in his book *Inspiration: Your Ultimate Calling*, describes the feeling of being inspired as:

"When you are inspired...you discover yourself to be a greater person by far than you ever dreamed yourself to be." [B]

That's a powerful statement. Imagine what *you* can do with your greater self.

Through my journey of writing this book and staying in touch with my power zone, I have had signs that I am on the right path and am using my greater self. These include overcoming obstacles and breaking through barriers I didn't think possible, having people show up at the right time to support me when I needed it, and others' powerful words igniting one more spark to keep going. All these signs kept my inspiration and passions turned on to follow through. They helped me stay tapped into my personal power zone to achieve my vision of success and publish this book.

When I am leading my life from my power zone, I am grounded, confident, powerful and energized, inspired and passionate. Things come so much easier, and I am not struggling and working against myself. I feel joyful, alive, aligned, and purposeful. I show up, meaning I embrace my greatness and "play bigger" in my life! I truly believe this comes from connecting with my most powerful self on the "inside" or what I call the Power Zone. How can you recognize this in yourself?

You may recognize it as I described, or when you feel your spirit, your core energy or personal truth deep inside of you. However it resonates with you is okay.

It's that knowledge that you are greater than any circumstance, fear, doubt, challenge, resistance, or obstacle. It's that center of your core energy connected to your values, where you feel empowered, calm, and peaceful.

The power zone is where transformation happens, courage is found, inspiration is fired up, passion and confidence combine, and taking risks to grow looks different. Are you feeling yours now?

The following are comments my clients have shared about how they feel when they are in touch with their power zone:

"I can see all my possibilities. I break through barriers I've set, and I am reminded of how valuable I am."

"I am not in a waffling state, I believe in myself, I harness my personal power, and I am more consistent and confident."

"I have less internal conflict, I practice a self-honoring approach and I feel in control of my life and my time."

"I live life by intention, I have increased enjoyment, feel successful, calm, productive, and satisfied. As a result, I am able to be present and believe and trust in myself."

In this state, the qualities of a confident woman are working for you and things become easier to deal with. It's easier to stand up for yourself and stay positive. You process things differently, allowing you to see other resolutions or possibilities that you might not have seen if you weren't tapped into your personal power.

The power zone presents great possibilities and has many benefits when you develop the ability to tap into yours.

You'll be consciously working to achieve your best; you'll be aware if you are showing up as your best self because you'll be living to your full potential, tapping into what makes you special. You'll have an improved quality of life because you'll feel purposeful, valuable, and able to make a difference, which naturally increases your success. You'll be able to stay focused on your true passionate goals, and as a result, shift from being just a task-doer to creating a legacy you can be proud of.

In the power zone, you can tap into your gifts, talents, and strengths to enable you to lead your life and to influence others to find their greatness, whether it is in your work or other areas of service. Your ability to tap into your personal power to align with what I call your "Power Zone" is to be cherished and developed.

How does it feel when you are NOT leading your life from your power zone?

Here is what a few of my clients say:

"Whatever my goal or desire is that I want to stretch to, I don't feel I can do it, or that I am even deserving of it."

"I worry more, have more negative self-talk, avoid failure, and am more resistant to change."

"I am in conflict with how I feel on the inside and how I am acting on the outside. I know better but I don't make the changes, at least not when I'm in this state."

"Because I am allowing it, I find I feel resentful and angry at myself. My self-worth is lowered, and it takes longer to get back in the zone."

When you are not working from your power zone, you end up feeling stuck or limited, or too accepting of how things are so you just settle for them. You struggle more with internal conflict because you are not honoring yourself. It is easier to lose sight of your gifts and talents; confidence and trust in yourself decrease. Your energy level is lower; you worry more and are less objective, since you're working below your capability. You're not able to powerfully lead others and you generally feel fragmented and disconnected from your life and dreams. You find yourself tolerating and most likely justifying or making excuses for problems. It's harder to use your strengths and talents to overcome challenges. In essence, you are suppressing your greatness.

Recognizing and tapping into your personal power zone is an essential life skill, one that will help you become a passionately empowered leader in all areas of your life.

Your thoughts make it difficult to do this because they can limit your ability to manifest what you desire for yourself. As a result, you can end up questioning your ability and your greatness. Lasting change involves recognizing and shifting your limiting thoughts and increasing your belief that you can create or become something different. If you can't imagine a different outcome, you are less likely to take the actions to create it. It is important to recognize this and practice removing all of your restricting ideas and beliefs. Pay attention to any negative thoughts creeping in that reflect ideas hampering you from manifesting your desires or dreams. Those are not coming from your power zone. Thoughts from your power zone are just that—powerful! They don't put boundaries or limits on what you intend to create for yourself in your life. They inspire you into action, excite you to stretch beyond your comfort zone, and motivate you to change your thinking or behaviors.

Ultimately, they connect the power in you with your purpose.

If you don't recognize and use the power you have or know how to tap into your power zone, you will have what I call "energy leaks." Your energy and power, which is really how you feel about yourself, shown in your thinking and related choices, isn't being used for you but is instead going out to other people's demands. As a result, you'll find yourself reacting to things and feeling resentful because you are not in the driver's seat of your life. I refer to this as "energy leaks" because you're allowing your energy to be leaked out to whatever comes your way. When you are working from your power zone, you value yourself and have more control over your choices so you have the ability to make more powerful choices for your life.

ഇൻന്ദ്ര

"If you realized how powerful your thoughts are, you would never think a negative thought."

—*Peace Pilgrim*

The Six Power Zone Principles™ to help you leave your comfort zone and lead your life from the power zone are:

Principle One

Design Your Vision of Success

Principle Two

Identify the Essential Risks

Principle Three

Create a Focus Action Plan

Principle Four

Overcome the Four Confidence Blockers

Principle Five

Understand the Qualities of a Confident Woman

Principle Six

Become an Empowered Leader

With the principles and processes in this book, you'll be able to celebrate your success and use the adaptable tools to start again with your next goal. As you create awareness and take action, your confidence and personal power will grow. Your results can go beyond your imagination and transform your life but will vary depending on your goals, how much effort you put into reaching them, and your ability to follow through.

I challenge you that it's perfectly fine to summon the courage required to venture away from your comfort zone and enter your power zone.

The rewards can be truly amazing when you start to let go of your limiting beliefs and replace them with a belief in your possibilities. Happiness and fulfillment come along with reaching your power zone, and you will start to realize that this type of personal power has always been inside you and just needed the right catalyst to bring it to fruition.

Let's get started with how to tap into your power zone using the first of the **Six Power Zone Principles™**!

Too often we don't dare reach beyond the day-to-day, past the status quos or confines of our comfort zone to get our share of all the personal success that awaits us.

Chapter One

Power Zone Principle #1

Design Your Vision of Success

> "You can't drive into the future if you are looking into a rear vision mirror."
> —Catherine DeVrye

Vision of Success

"Some people dream of worthy accomplishments, while others stay awake and do them." —Unknown

At the beginning of 2006, I was well on my way to launching a new and exciting business plan. By the summer, I was fully engaged and had used every resource and all my creative energy to succeed. Then in July, I got some serious news about my youngest daughter's health that changed the amount of time and energy I could dedicate to implementing my vision.

I have to admit that I take pride in being a mother and, at the time, a single mother for many years. The news meant that I had to adjust my focus, suspend some projects and slow down the momentum I had worked so hard to gain. Of course, any mother would do what she could for her child. I wanted to find a way to continue fulfilling my passion, not give up, and provide my family with a strong and positive future.

That wasn't an easy task with the many hours I needed to devote to finding new resources, seeing to my daughter's needs, and the big one—not working during these periods. Additionally, I had to find a way to accommodate her special needs into my vision and to allow more self-care for me at the same time.

Honestly, I had to find a way to embrace and not resent my new situation with its challenges and responsibilities. Life has a way of presenting us with mixed blessings, and I thought this one couldn't have come at a worse time.

With the help of a dear friend and fellow coach, I went through the process of change to accept and release my own fears and was able to see that I could find a way. I eventually found hidden gifts in my situation, although I couldn't see them at first.

Because I had a clear written vision of what I wanted to achieve and I strongly believed it was my personal mission to do so, I found resources I hadn't thought of.

I built stronger, collaborative relationships, communicated more clearly, allowed more support, and, once again, broadened my comfort zone and developed my resiliency to change.

Because I knew where I wanted to go, I could exercise more patience with my progress, see new opportunities to make it happen and adjust to support my daughter, while keeping the larger vision in mind.

Learning to stretch towards my vision while being flexible enough to adapt has helped me continue my progress on my journey to success, in spite of any obstacles I may face. This life lesson showed me how to stay tapped into my power zone, draw on my strengths and talents, and keep the bigger belief in who I am and my life purpose alive!

What is the moral of this story?

Life is a journey to success, but what do you want your success to look like? What are you willing to do, or how will you allow yourself to grow to reach that success?

Without a vision, the faith and trust necessary to sustain you during difficult times isn't always there. Without a vision, it's difficult to know where to go next.

In life, most people spend more time planning vacations and holidays than they do their own lives. There are so many things fighting for our attention on a daily basis that it becomes challenging to step off the hamster wheel and take charge of our own experiences.

However, in today's competitive and ever-changing business environment, average thoughts and actions won't do! To get ahead in your business or career and be a leader in your life, it is imperative that you have your vision and take a stand on what you believe.

This can be challenging as a professional woman; perhaps you are a mother, a wife, or a caretaker, being pulled in many directions and yet you are still expected to fulfill your responsibilities in all areas.

That is why it's important to tap into your power zone through your vision of success and by being a leader, taking intelligent risks to take charge, starting first with your own life. Furthermore, in order to help others, embrace risks in inevitable times of change, it's more necessary than ever to set the example by expanding your own comfort zone. Having a solid personal vision enables you to take intelligent risks to grow, by creating focus in the areas you want to expand or work on.

Creating a Vantage Point

Having a clear vision allows you to approach challenges from a different "vantage point," a different perspective of what actions or information will support your goals and where it is best to exert your energies, such as:

Dealing with information overload – You can compare your vision against the large volume of information you have coming at you, like emails and advertising offers, and determine more quickly if that information will support your vision or not. If it does, you can prioritize when and how to use it based on where you are in the steps, you're taking to achieve your vision of success.

Decision making and use of time—Once you identify the values important to you, you can incorporate these into your decisions and see if you are honoring your values or not. This can make it easier to set boundaries and let go of tasks that don't fit your vision. The same idea applies to other activities, like networking or joining an organization. Ask yourself if your decisions fit your vision and how meaningful they are.

Opening up to other methods and avoiding tunnel vision—If you are clear about your vision then you can be receptive to additional methods or means you didn't know would make your vision possible because you can focus on the big picture and not be stuck on the idea that there's only one way to get there. Rather, you trust in the overall vision and can relax, making you more responsive to more possibilities.

Telling whether you're on track—A vision makes it easier to track results, to determine if ideas will work or not, and to correct your course more effectively.

If you know where you're going and can communicate that confidently, clearly and passionately, there's no limit to, how far you can go or how far people will follow you. This will also open the door to new contacts and affiliations, as well as to new opportunities to collaborate.

For example, one of the key things I did was to include into my vision the desire to seek opportunities to practice sharing my personal story and why I am so passionate about what I do. After putting my intention out there, I had the opportunity to speak at a yearly kick-off meeting for a women-in-business organization. In emphasizing my personal message of the importance of taking risks and the lessons learned in doing so, I experienced this phenomenon: if you are passionate and communicate that passion, people will follow and want to help you.

At past speaking engagements, audience members had routinely come up to me and shared their thoughts, but this time was different. From their reactions, I knew I had reached them on an individual level—eyes full of energy and belief, mile-wide smiles, and "I can relate" nods. And the most satisfying yet most humbling result was seeing people lining up to have a chance to talk with me.

I realized their reactions affirmed I was on the right track. The sacrifices I made by taking time out for my daughter, trusting that my vision would happen even if I had to go about it a little differently, being willing to take a risk and share more of my personal story, had all come full circle. I felt so enriched.

I had manifested this experience by setting the intention by including it in my New Year's vision statement that I set each year: *I am a leader of personal transformation defined by making a difference in the lives of others through my work.* By making the commitment, I began to take purposeful steps to make my vision manifest. I wasn't quite where I desired to be when I started that year, but visions are intended to draw us into action, out of our current state, our comfort zone, and begin to bring our desires, passions, gifts, talents, and dreams to life.

Making the Commitment

As a professional woman, you have plenty of day-to-day experience getting things done because that's what you have to do (especially if you are a parent). You show up at the office, the meeting, or to your own business and get to work. Then the cycle continues as you go home and assume your role there as well.

Too often we don't dare reach beyond the day-to-day, past the status quos or confines of our comfort zone to get our share of all the personal success that awaits us. Notice the word "awaits." Your desired outcomes, results, and life changes are awaiting you.

One of the reasons we can't reach our personal success is we don't feel we have the time to even think about what opportunities we want next. I understand, as I have fallen into this thinking trap before. However, staying in this quagmire of limiting belief results in our having to step back and figure out what we are working toward or what we want from life, even after we have already started down a path. This can generate extra work, frustration and even create panic as we wonder how we're going to get back to where we desire to be or how we'll get everything accomplished. Unfortunately, living in the comfort zone makes us less likely to take risks and so we don't try; we stay where we are. And as I said earlier, our tolerance increases until it becomes natural, resulting in a habit that is hard to change.

Moreover, we may find ourselves just daydreaming of great things, desiring them, and perhaps telling ourselves we will do something–in the future–to get there. Most often, these internal whispers lack commitment and consistent action to reveal their full glory.

Merely dreaming and aspiring for something more is a passive place to start, which won't necessarily produce the appropriate actions or point you in a clear direction to get to the next level of happiness and personal success.

For this to happen, we must make a personal commitment of what we want our future to be like. That means putting it in writing and then making a conscious effort to bring your thoughts and actions into alignment with it. I am not talking about a to-do list either!

Often I hear professional women refer to their calendars, day planners, projects or to-do lists as accomplishing their desires or vision. Usually what they are really referring to are the goals and tasks they want or need to achieve or perform. Whether or not this complements their vision is another story.

Key Point—A goal and any supporting task are NOT the same as having your personal vision of success!

Think of it like this: Your vision is the description of what it would be like to fulfill your untapped possibilities and realize your life purpose. Certain goals and tasks are the stepping stones you'll walk across to get there.

If you build a pathway with stepping stones full of to-do's, have to's, or someone else's want to's, you end up in a place you don't recognize. You look around and wonder how you ever got here, who these people are, and who you are. You'll only find yourself further away from your vision and it might even be so far off in the distance you just can't see it ever being a reality. It then becomes a wishful dream.

In this example, you could end up feeling disconnected, fragmented, and uneasy. You lack a sense of accomplishment because deep inside you know this doesn't fit who you are. This depletes your motivating energy and leaves you feeling like it's not enough. As a result, you'll end up trying to do more to fill the void, because you're not connected with that desired feeling, and any sense of progress and confidence you are on right path will be an illusion.

You must have a clear vision in order to see the path you'll take on your journey to success.

The strategy to tap into this Power Zone Principle is:

Your Vision of Success (You may have heard it described before as a personal mission) is the first strategy to set you on your journey to success.

So you begin this process by designing a vision that is exciting, purposeful and fulfilling, that will inspire you to achieve it.

With the creation of your Vision of Success statement, you'll focus your energy and move toward what you want, and then you'll use the principles and strategies in here to fully manifest it.

You'll create your **Vision of Success statement** by defining the things that are most important to you – **your values**, how you want to **be of service** in the world, what **makes you special**, the **legacy you want** to leave behind, and your most essential **true goals**.

Keep in mind this is not a business vision or mission statement. These are structured differently. I have used a modified version of this exercise, to support business owners and team leaders as they tap into their leadership power zones so they can, as one client said, "not just show up to work, but rather work to fulfill a meaningful vision." The difference it made in her organization, team, and personal life was transforming.

No matter where you currently are in your life, whether you have a personal vision or not, don't skip this part!

"A mission could be defined as the image of a desired state that you want to get to. Once fully seen, it will inspire you to act, fuel your motivation, and determine your behaviour."   —*Charles Garfield*

Part 1: Values

As a professional woman, who you are becoming is just as important as what you are doing.

When you can honor your values as you contribute to and interact with the world around you, you're able to express who you really are. You will find this much more fulfilling for you and it will allow you to tap into your deepest potential and your most powerful source of energy.

Emotional energy, not mental energy, is the true motivator of the human spirit. Emotional energy has its source in what people believe and value. Values give meaning to life. When there is alignment between your values and your actions, you'll find you are able to tap into your deepest level of creativity, take more strengthening risks and increase your success.

Values are essential to define and consider when you're planning to create success; they're the principles you're choosing to live by. They're different than morals, which may have been taught or instilled in you as you grew up. Values are inherent within you and may, unfortunately, be very different from how you actually live.

Let me clarify that morals can be looked upon as the standards of good and bad, which govern an individual's behavior and choices. These may derive from society and government, religion, or self. They are, in essence, the standards by which you judge yourself and others. An example would be your view on marriage versus cohabitation.

Values can be looked upon as standards or qualities considered worthwhile and desirable. Value is a concept that describes the beliefs of an individual or culture. An example of not living one's values or beliefs would be advocating a healthy lifestyle while not exercising or making other healthy lifestyle choices for oneself.

When your decisions and actions go against your fundamental values, it creates an internal conflict that affects your desire and willingness to take action. It also causes stress and low energy. This is particularly evident in our work lives, where we spend such a major percentage of our time.

The Tolerance Factor

I once had a client who, after years of climbing up the corporate ladder, came to me, not celebrating her successes as you would imagine, but feeling guilty and unfulfilled. Though on the outside she appeared to be successful, she couldn't understand why she wasn't engaged and deploying her talents fully, and she wondered how she ever ended up where she was, daydreaming and wishing for something else.

This is what I call the "Tolerance Factor." After years of ignoring the promptings of her true self, she built up a tolerance that went against her values. Moreover, with each denial of expressing her true self, she further reinforced the acceptance of the belief "this is how it is and always has to be." It's sad to witness the driving core energy and the higher self being suppressed and losing its vibrancy.

Another client who owned her own business came to the realization that she had unintentionally taken on her father's business. Consequently, it wasn't her passion, it was his, and this caused conflict in her energy, killed her desire to work, and put a strain on her relationships. Her day-to-day work wasn't honoring her core values. With over 10 years invested in someone else's dreams, she made the courageous decision to take a big risk, go back to school and pursue her true desires. Periodically, she will still check in and share her enthusiasm about her decision to honor herself.

Alternately, I have worked with clients who *are* living their passion, in their careers or business. They make it happen by finding ways to express themselves in their work and in areas of service, and because they are aligned with their values, they have a clear vision of the success they want to create.

With no excuses, no guilt and with what seems like luck, these people manifest the opportunities to continue finding ways to reveal their desires. It is not luck; it is personal discipline, willingness and courage to lead life from their personal power zone, to stay in tune with what they intend to create.

Being part of the powerful transformation of leaving the comfort zone and claiming your power zone is why I do what I do. I feel honored to be living a life path that affords me the opportunity to participate in helping my clients claim their greatness.

ℰᏡᏟᎡ

Making choices that support your values is essential to tapping into your power zone and your long-term happiness. That's why it's essential to integrate your values into your Vision of Success statement.

Begin by looking over this list of common values:

Accomplishment	Joy
Abundance	Leadership
Achievement	Loyalty
Adventure	Nature
Altruism	Openness
Autonomy	Orderliness
Beauty	Personal Growth
Balance	Partnership
Clarity	Physical Appearance
Commitment	Power
Communication	Privacy
Community	Professionalism
Connecting to Others	Recognition
Creativity	Respect
Emotional Health	Romance
Environment	Security
Excellence	Self-Care
Family	Self-Expression
Flexibility Freedom	Self-Mastery
Friendship	Self-Realization
Fulfillment	Service
Fun	Spirituality
Holistic Living	Trust
Honesty	Truth
Humor	Vitality
Integrity	Walking the Talk
Intimacy	

Now choose the top five values that are most important to you, the ones that would be most beneficial if integrated fully into your personal and professional life. List them in the spaces below.

LIST 1: My Top 5 Values

1._____

2._____

3._____

4._____

5._____

Part 2: Being of Service

The line between business and social/environmental philosophies is becoming less defined in today's world.

As businesses strive to demonstrate their social consciousness, individuals are also feeling a similar awakening. For some, it's no longer enough to merely succeed in the conventional ways (financial and material). More people are committing themselves to making a difference in the world and realizing their own unique life purpose.

We're more concerned and aware of our connection to the world around us, and we want to serve, not just take. It is by giving back that our human spirit feels most connected to the world.

Each one of us knows individuals who have inspired us by their contributions. It could be a mentor, a celebrity, a neighbor, a colleague, a family member, or a friend. These people inspire us because they are living outside the normal boundaries of their comfort zone and are making a difference in spite of their everyday life events and responsibilities.

My own experience of service

Personally, being of service is a big part of where I am today. From a very young age, I felt I had something bigger than myself to do. It wasn't always clear what it was but I felt it was so. If you read stories about people making a difference, generally they will share the same belief of feeling the calling of their purpose or the passion about the areas where they wanted to make a difference.

The awareness grew from each opportunity to serve and empower others to make their own self-discoveries, such as finding their belief in themselves as they move through tough situations, or claiming their strength to do things they once thought impossible. I feel my most inspiring and powerful energy when I am serving and doing my life work–coaching. This cannot happen without being grounded and clear on my purpose.

I first released an earlier version of this book as an e-book in 2006. After receiving feedback and personal stories of how it inspired others to take risks to "show up" and claim who they are or what they want, and the transforming results they had from applying these principles, I thought about how to broaden its reach and publish a printed edition. Writing a book takes a tremendous amount of effort, time, and energy and requires personal sacrifices to take on such an endeavor. So why would I want to do that with everything else already on my plate? Because I felt a burning calling to help others.

How I would fulfill it I didn't know yet.

One of the qualities of being a confident woman is being resourceful, being willing to seek out support and information that can help you. I inherited this quality from my mother. I never ceased to be amazed by her ability to serve and fulfill the needs of her six children with limited resources. While growing up, I recall how my mother invented 101 ways to use hamburger and turn hand-me-downs into the latest fashion with a needle and thread and a decorative application. She was creative with stretching out the life of so many things and teaching us kids how to get the most out of what we had and when we couldn't get anymore, how to use our imagination to look beyond it. This skill came in very handy when I was a single parent trying to make ends meet and to stay hopeful in spite of sometimes meager situations.

Armed with this quality of resourcefulness, I set out to seek the information I needed to go about turning my intentions into realities.

One morning, while going through my emails, I read a weekly subscription newsletter. I enjoyed reading these but never reached out to the author since I figured she was too busy to respond. However, that morning I was filled with this urge to further my goal, so I felt compelled to make my intentions known. I sent an email and asked for some advice, hoping, if nothing else, to send out a positive affirmation to the universe to support my bigger vision. I have to admit part of me accepted I may not hear back, though I tried to reframe those thoughts into trust, keeping my hopes open that at least I was moving forward and looking for answers and direction.

Then, to my surprise, I received a reply. I was thrilled, especially since it came with a bonus: an invitation to speak.

The lesson here is that there is a universal energy of success and prosperity that wants to provide what we need to serve.

We just need to ask for it and take actions to make it happen.

By putting out my desire to serve, I manifested an opportunity to have a conversation with Milana Leshinsky, author of "Coaching Millions." I felt she was a kindred spirit with her driving passion. Although Milana's book is packed with business strategies, she also shares her own personal story of triumphing over adversity, learning to be open to attracting ways to serve, and having the painstaking diligence to stay the course when it didn't seem possible.

The conversation was energizing and exciting because she understood me. I could be authentic in my passion, and it was fun to brainstorm. I'll admit that at first when she told me, "I could listen to you for hours, René. You have a special energy, and you need to get that out there," I thought, I am no one famous or special so who am I to be so bold and write a book? Her encouragement and the belief of those close to me increased my confidence and affirmed that I had something to offer. I became convinced it was my responsibility to get my ideas "out there," and why shouldn't it be through a book?

By using several of my own strategies, I was able to be resourceful and find ways to make it all work. During the course of writing this book and launching my supporting program, Power Zone Mastery™, I also practiced reserving time for filling up my self-care reservoir, which you'll learn about in Principle #4 later in the book. And I've stayed true to my goal of dispelling the number one myth: confident women have all the answers. NOT! I asked for and allowed support from many in order to reach my vision of success.

I am often reminded that one person does not build great things by themselves; it takes the support and service of others. You too, can make great things happen. They won't happen overnight, but they can't happen at all if you don't design your vision and begin to take actions to fulfill it. So here is your turn to make a difference. Envision leaving your comfort zone and creating and aligning with the support of others. Where do you want to serve?

LIST 2: Making a Difference

List 3-5 ways that you would like to make a difference in the world. If that seems too big, think of ways you can support your community or the parts of the world you interact with.

1._____

2._____

3._____

4._____

5._____

Part 3: Being Special

> "*Our deepest fear is not that we are inadequate. Our deepest fear is that we are powerful beyond measure. It is our light, not our darkness, that frightens us.*"
>
> —*Marianne Williamson, in "A Return To Love"*

What if you were told you had the key to unlock your potential anytime you wanted. Would you use it?

Actually, your personal power, what makes you special, is available to unlock at anytime; it never really goes away. It is only diminished by your own self-doubt. You choose to believe and tap into your personal power, to live your life from your power zone or not.

You always have a choice, and through choice you CAN "design" your life! It's much easier to make choices to claim your life when you are working from your power zone. It doesn't matter what your past has been, where you are today, or that you are a woman, you can make powerful things happen in your life. You can fulfill your service goals and you can achieve your career or business aspirations.

Women are no longer limited by society's conventions that told us where we belong in business or in the world. We only limit ourselves. Want proof?

In 2008 we had a historic presidential campaign, and regardless of where you stood politically, this was evidence that a powerful shift was taking place. We had one woman seeking to be president of the United States of America, and another seeking to vice president! Our history as women has now been forever altered, and as a result, the validity of a glass ceiling will be challenged.

Can you imagine having the type of confidence to run for the highest offices? What would you do with that much confidence? Without a doubt, this has to be one of the most courageous goals I've seen taken on by a man or woman.

Through these two women's beliefs in themselves, and the countless examples of other courageous women throughout history who have taken risks to claim their gifts, passions, and personal power, more women will be encouraged to find what makes them special and go after what it takes to make a difference.

How will you show up?

What makes you special isn't measured by how famous you become or whether you'll have an impact on history. It is measured by who you are on the inside and how much confidence you have to express it on the outside.

Inside every woman is <u>her most powerful self</u>, her personal greatness, just waiting to emerge!

I teach my clients that to discover their personal power means to claim their true selves, their gifts, strengths, talents and inner qualities, in spite of the circumstances or challenges they may face.

This is what I refer to as "Showing Up 100 Percent" and leading your life from your power zone, so that YOU, and the world you influence and affect, can benefit from your uniqueness.

What truths do you have waiting to be discovered? What passion or internal desire could you and those around you benefit from? What truth about yourself can you find or what truth have you been hiding? I hope to inspire you to challenge yourself to Show Up.

In a nutshell, we all have the opportunity to define, celebrate, and make use of our special gifts. By applying this step, you will learn how to make the most of what makes you special.

LIST 3: List 3-5 things that you believe make you special.

1._____

2._____

3._____

4._____

5._____

If you have a hard time with this step, think about what your friends or family say. What do they refer to when they speak about your gifts and talents? What do they see in you that you are not claiming? Catch yourself if you start to make excuses or let limiting beliefs creep into your thinking. Challenge yourself here. Will you recreate what you have or will you stop clinging to the walls of your comfort zone? The world is waiting for your powerful self to say, "I am here!"

You only have one life. Make it powerful. Make your energy count.

Part 4: Creating a Legacy

Your world, and ultimately your legacy, are defined by you, and this includes your personal and professional contributions. My own goal is not to change the world but positively influence the parts I interact with. In order to manifest this, I have to know what that positive interaction looks like. How else would I know if I am achieving my goal?

Life is not defined by being an almighty task-doer.

Many things prevent us from looking beyond the everyday pressures of life to envision what the future will look like or to take the appropriate steps to create it.

I have helped clients come to the wonderful discovery that their life is not defined by being an almighty task-doer. They can create the legacy they want to leave behind each and every day. If you find yourself coming to this realization, don't feel pressured or guilty; your awakening can ignite freedom, hope, purpose and possibility.

Through self-awareness, you can begin to shift and change course. Keep in mind this won't happen overnight. You are rooted in habits, beliefs, fears and obligations that consume your time. But the seasons of your life change, and you will have the opportunity to decide how you will enjoy the next season. And just like planning for a trip, you can get excited about the potential to set sail on a new adventure, envision it, set the intention, and take the initial steps to prepare, and eventually you will be boldly plotting a new course for yourself.

Keep in mind that this requires patience and determination. It also necessitates belief in yourself and knowing that you are worth leaving a mark, in essence, your legacy.

The sad truth about being a passenger in your life

The principle of having a vision made a huge difference in what my life could have looked like. I realized I had a tool that helped me serve others without giving up on my goals and dreams.

This helped me approach life in a *self-honoring* way that allowed me to get in the driver's seat of my life and see clearly what I realistically could and could not do. It empowered me to say the biggest guilt-driven words in the professional woman's vocabulary...No Thank You!

By using this tool, I could stop piecing myself out and give my best self to what was most important to me, while still having energy left to choose where I could be the most helpful and effective. I could stop being a task-doer and start creating a legacy. Having a vision I could refer to and make decisions by influenced me in many ways, as I know it can influence you, too. Consider the following contrasts.

Which category do you fall in?

Here are some characteristics of women who DON'T have a vision to guide their life:

- Are not willing to face the things that are taking them away from what they really want
- Put blinders on hoping that will make it go away
- Wish things would change, disappear or dissolve by themselves
- Find themselves wondering when enough is enough
- Are in conflict with their life and work
- Find it hard to be in the moment and feel joy versus guilt
- Focus more on driving someone else's vision forward
- Feel like their life is on autopilot
- Do too much of the should do's, versus the want to's

In contrast, women who HAVE a vision benefit through the following:

- Generate the change they want
- Are in the driver's seat of their life with hands firmly on the wheel
- Design their future by defining what they want and taking initiative
- Have the power to choose
- Increase personal freedom
- Create balance and focus on the things they want
- Stay in touch with their personal greatness
- Are confident in their ability to have a fulfilling future
- Find it easier to make decisions and use their time wisely

Designing our own Vision of Success statement is your next exercise. This will help you begin with the end in mind and allow you to use the process in this book to make changes from within, ones that ignite your personal passion. With the tools in the next sections, you'll be able to design the appropriate steps to make your vision a reality.

Exercise: Imagine that you are retiring from your current business or career. An auditorium is full of people who have gathered to celebrate and honor you. Someone is walking up to the podium, preparing to give a speech outlining all you have contributed, personally and professionally, to the world around you.

Take time now to write that speech and then list the top 3-5 things that you are most proud to leave behind. If this seems too big, envision your life a year from now and write a declaration of what you have accomplished.

Take a deep breath and get somewhere comfortable. Let go of seeing things as you are today, let go of the need to be perfect or to have the knowledge of how you will achieve it, just S-T-R-E-T-C-H out of your comfort zone and let your creativity and passions come alive.

LIST 4: Take a look at your legacy and list 3-5 achievements you'd be most proud of

1._____

2._____

3._____

4._____

5._____

Part 5: True Goals

Take a look at the list from your legacy exercise and carefully consider whether those accomplishments are things that you really want (True Goals) or whether they're things you think you should want.

The energy attached to "should want" goals is draining energy. Rather than driving you forward, these wants diminish your power, decrease your motivation and stall your progress.

Instead, when you connect with the "really want" goals, you feel that internal desire and a higher energy level. You may recognize that feeling as being in your Power Zone. You feel alive, connected, assured, balanced and unstoppable.

Did you list any of those accomplishments that stirred up the possibilities laying dormant in your power zone?

You feel alive, connected, assured, balanced and unstoppable.

When you find your true goals – the ones filled with passion that you focus on to fulfill your potential – you have an energy that radiates from you and inspires others. These are not peripheral goals, meaning the day-to-day, go to work, go to the meeting, do the paperwork type of goals that will keep you in the status quo. Those types of goals can't raise you to the next level of success. It's important to identify the True Goals that will make the biggest difference in your journey to success.

We'll discuss further how to identify if your goals will motivate you and how to establish a clearly defined goal in Principle #3. For now, check and see if you need to remake your list.

REVISED LIST 4: List 3-5 achievements I'd be most proud of (my legacy)

1._____

2._____

3._____

4._____

5._____

ଏଠଓଷ

"To come to be you must have a vision of Being, a Dream, a Purpose, a Principle. You will become what your vision is." —*Peter Nivio Zarlenga*

Building Your Vision of Success Statement

Here is where you need to let go of the all-or-nothing thinking. Not everything has to be in place: let go of past obstacles or failures. Trust yourself so you can laser in with this process. You will be working to initially create a more concise Vision of Success statement to make it easier to shift your thinking and desires and begin taking action.

Choose the most important item from each of your four lists right now and circle it.

Now complete the following paragraph:

To honor my value of_____

(circled item from list #1)

I will_____

(circled item from list #4)

Using my_____

(circled item from list #3)

To achieve_____

 (circled item from list #2)

My example: To honor my value of personal growth, I will offer a book of my most successful coaching strategies, using my creativity, to achieve the empowerment of professional women everywhere.

Though this is a small statement compared to all you have identified in the exercises, you can look at this and easily determine where you can get started to create your focus in each of the key elements: values, service, being special, true goals, and set a plan to get there.

For example, I set a goal to honor my value of personal growth by writing this book and letting my personality and stories come out through creativity, which allowed me to illustrate possibilities and empower you to design and reach for your own vision of success.

NOTE: Hang on to the list of items that you didn't choose. You'll revisit those when it's time to begin the process again. You might want to come back to something and focus on it later. You may need to adjust yours to work for you. Sometimes the statement won't be clear because you are in conflict with one of the items in your list, perhaps because you're afraid to claim it or are not pulling in the right one. Try to choose the one area to focus on that will make the biggest difference and get you moving.

The key here is to not use all the items from your list, since that could make you feel overwhelmed and stall you from taking action. In this section, you are working first to create a brief statement of what is most important for you to reach today, so you can start to laser in and take action towards achieving it.

As you build confidence while working towards your vision, you can eventually broaden your statement, pulling in additional items from your list, adding the lifestyle you wish to live, the money you desire to make, the relationships you wish to foster and so forth, designing an all-encompassing statement. For now, consistency is key while integrating the vision into your life a little at a time.

If you already have a personal vision or mission statement, compare yours to the key elements we discussed in this section and add or make any adjustments that will help you leave your current comfort zone.

Tip: Write or type out your "Vision of Success Statement." You can even illustrate it to make it even more inspiring and powerful and post it somewhere so that you'll see it often. Better yet, read it every morning to frame your day and attract the opportunities to fulfill it!

Years ago I had a picture taken of me in front of my dream car with the keys in my hand. I put the picture on my desk and I found that I began to create focus, which allowed me to save up for the down payment. On January 4, 2004, I bought my Audi TT roadster convertible. The reason I was so excited I could do this was because I was practicing the law of attraction and had set this as a reward for achieving my larger vision of success at the time, when I was a single parent, finishing my coaching education and just starting my own business. I knew that to be able to accomplishment this would demonstrate my ability to use my vision to set goals and see them through. I still have the car, and whenever I want to feel that sense of personal power or want to celebrate success, I take the top down, put on some good tunes and take a drive. It is a great reminder that when there is a will, there's a way!

I have continued to use this method to create focus on my bigger goals and attract success into my business and personal life. I have my Vision of Success on the wall over my computer so I can see it and read it every day. It helps me stay grounded. I mean it and deserve it, and so do you!

Here are a few favorite benefits my clients have shared from using a vision to shape their life:

"I am anchored in new beliefs of what is possible and feel less turmoil with making decisions. I get excited at the day's possibilities."

"Using a vision has allowed me to build up my believability in what is possible; then by focusing on this, my courage to pursue my vision increased."

"I could finally release my fears of claiming my true self and I worked from a place of confidence that has resulted in increased mental energy and positive momentum towards my vision."

"I am more open to reassessment and new discoveries, and through this, I've been able to create an exciting and fulfilling life."

Vision Wrap Up:

Ultimately, your vision is much more than a statement of what you want to achieve. It's the result of an inner exploration of what's important to you and how you want to feel about what you've accomplished. Your vision should allow you to see, feel, and believe in a new you!

When you work and live according to a vision, it's easier to make decisions because each choice is either something that will lead you closer to your vision of success or not. It will help you pace yourself and acknowledge your progress. You'll see a bigger picture outside of your current situation and be able to set deadlines and increase your personal accountability to follow through. When you are working to fulfill your vision, you'll feel excited and purposeful, and your creative juices will be flowing as you become a "change factor" in your life!

Without a vision, you may either be watching life and success pass you by as things happen to you, or you may be working furiously to make things happen, constantly juggling and reacting to everyday events.

With a vision, you have a plan and you're proactively working to fulfill it, assessing and reassessing as you act with confidence. You can't hit a target you can't see!

With the creation of your vision and applying the Power Zone Principles, you'll finally understand why you can't seem to make things happen, why you may lose faith, or why you may get distracted and not stay the course, or why others don't seem to know how to support you.

One key principle of manifesting your vision of success statement will be creating your Focus Action Plan that we will outline in a later chapter, to align your goals and actions that will lead you to your vision.

Chapter Two

Power Zone
Principle #2

Identify the Essential Risks

"When women take the risk to be their most powerful self, they are stronger than any fear or doubt they may face."

—René Johnson

What's Risk Got To Do With It?

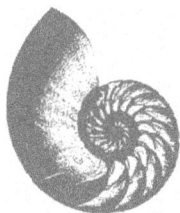

"A woman is like a teabag…you never know how strong she is until you put her in hot water."

—Eleanor Roosevelt

Fulfilling your vision of success requires that you develop the confidence to take risks. In this case, a risk is an opportunity to shift your thinking and stretch out of your comfort zone. It's the willingness to try a new behavior or a different thinking style. The more risks we take, the higher our chances are of being successful. The more personal success we experience, the more confidence we will have to stay on course in our journey to success.

I'm guessing you may feel comfortable where you are now, so anywhere you go from here involves the risk that where you end up might not be as comfortable. That's why many women never achieve their peak potential for success: they opt for comfort instead of risk.

When we work to expand our comfort zone by taking risks to grow, we are able to create bigger goals and take bolder steps. When we work from a place of confidence instead of comfort, we connect with our strengths and talents, our self-belief is strong, and our creative energy and passions are alive because we are working from our personal power zone.

In our power zone, our decision making is different, our willingness to try new behaviors and thinking styles is increased, and the opportunities to achieve our goals become more tangible. We are much more open to taking risks to grow from the inside out. In fact, we welcome opportunities for selfexploration!

When you are <u>not</u> working from your power zone, you may feel overwhelmed, you resist change, and your fears grow stronger. Because of this, you want to stay in your comfort zone and think everything through, rationalize, and eventually limit your chances for change and increased happiness and success.

At first, staying in your comfort zone feels safe and even more natural than to risk stepping into your power zone. I get it; I've been there before! However, this is what I call an energy drainer, because it takes so much more energy to cling to our comfort zone than to step out of it. It really does.

Once we summon the courage to tap into our power zone and feel our greatness, it ignites and radiates within us. When we put our greatness aside by not claiming it and not leading our life from it, an internal battle begins. We are left to choose between shifting away from what holds us back versus choosing to claim our greatness and our possibilities by "showing up" 100 percent. In your lifetime, I bet you have felt this internal conflict, and I'm sure you can recognize the push and pull, and the draining energy I'm referring to.

It's an illusion created by your fears that you can simply ignore the personal greatness stirring inside you. This greatness is always there, and you either use your energy to fulfill your vision and make a difference, or you use your energy to avoid, ignore, justify, deny and or otherwise suppress purposeful thoughts and actions.

Once we summon the courage to tap into our power zone and feel our greatness, it ignites and radiates within us.

Why, then, if it doesn't go away, do we tend to suppress our potential and create so much more work and conflict for ourselves? Because most people don't like to take risks. It's uncomfortable. It's dangerous. It's even scary.

Indeed, risks can have negative outcomes, but in many cases, the cost of not taking risks and staying in your comfort zone with no hope for a more exciting, rewarding and fulfilling future is a far more negative outcome than that of any risk you may take.

I look at risk as a friend, a companion on my road to success, a necessary ingredient to ensure that my success is welldeserved, appreciated and long-lasting.

People say that the bigger the risk, the greater the reward, and it's true. When you show the world that you are willing to take the risks necessary to become successful and take actions that are in line with your core beliefs, things begin working out in your favor. Serendipitous events begin happening, all because of the presence of your companion: risk.

Our sticky feet hold us down

Traditionally, men have been encouraged to engage in a wide variety of risk-taking endeavors and have had more opportunities to do so. On the other hand, women are encouraged to conform and play by the rules, not to take risks or challenge established societal norms. But that holds us back and doesn't allow us to work from our power zone so we can share the unique gifts we have to offer as women. It's time to change this for your own benefit!

Now, more than ever, women are well poised to break through the cultural and gender stereotypes and more importantly, to change their own behavior traits and limiting beliefs. In fact, I would argue that our limiting beliefs <u>are the number one reason</u> we hold ourselves back. As a result, we haven't allowed ourselves to receive all the success we could possibly handle.

I find it exciting that today more and more women are choosing to overcome these barriers and start their own businesses or break the glass ceiling in their career. We CAN change our behavior and challenge our limiting beliefs. It's not the glass ceiling or lack of opportunity but our own sticky feet, made up of our limiting beliefs, that holds us down.

As a woman business owner and coach of women in business, I've seen that no matter how successful we as women get, we all eventually hit the edge of our comfort zone, and can't grow anymore unless we're willing to take new risks.

For some, this zone is smaller than for others. The learned behavior of conformity, combined with the self-limiting beliefs we've adopted over the years can hold us back from taking even the smallest of risks.

What exactly is standing between you and unrecognized possibilities? Whether it's fear, limiting beliefs, a lack of assertiveness or unhealthy habits and behaviors, those things will all be challenged as you apply the principles I'm advocating here.

Don't let thoughts of change concern you so much that you're immobilized. You've been thinking about change for a while, but now you're ready to do more than just think about your dreams; you're ready to create what you really want.

Consider these thoughts to make the process easier:

We all know that change isn't always easy, and I understand that you may not want to let go of some of these long-held behaviours right away. All you need to remember is that you keep an open mind and keep thinking of the big picture. Whatever you associate with success – whether it's your retirement dreams, travel plans, family fun, personal fulfillment, mentoring and giving back, or simply celebrating your legacy – keep those things in mind when change seems too difficult to undertake.

When you begin a system of change, it might seem everything you're asked to do is "work." What my coaching clients and I have experienced is that gradually our desire to make necessary changes increases until we strive to actually make them. And, eventually, you'll love this system because you'll see positive results and feel the transformation taking place.

No change will ever occur if you don't get to the root cause of the problem. You can make short gains through the use of pure willpower, but you will always be fighting the proverbial vicious cycle, and the problem will keep popping back up and challenging any changes you've tried to make.

Changing your limiting thoughts and associated behaviors is the only way you'll get different and lasting results! My goal is to empower you to connect your inner purpose and passion residing in your power zone to your outer goals and tasks.

Changing your limiting thoughts and associated behaviors is the only way you'll get different and lasting results!

Summoning my own courage to change

I know firsthand the challenges faced by a woman like you, who refuses to take the easy road or settle for the norm, and who desires to be passionate and purposeful in her life and work.

Professional women like you should be inspired to find and express their full potential, to choose a life of powerful intentions instead of living life by default.

When women take the risk to be their most powerful self, they are stronger than any fear or doubt they may face. I can personally relate because of the risks I've taken in my own life. I have constantly continued to work to conquer my fears and overcome obstacles to go after my goals and dreams. It doesn't mean every choice has been powerful or correct, or that I haven't had to start over a few times. There have been times when I felt quite hopeless.

My journey has required me to discover a great belief in myself, as yours will of you. I have faced the challenge many times to take intelligent risks, summon courage, and not allow limiting beliefs to keep me in my comfort zone. I have had to hold true to the possibilities that stirred up inside me.

That hasn't always been easy to do, considering some of the circumstances I've had to face. One very difficult circumstance involved the ultimate decision of life and death, safety versus harm, and stretching my comfort zone in a profound way.

In 1994, as the mother of two young daughters, I was faced with making a life-defining choice. What made this even more difficult was that I had lost contact with friends and all my family members because of the abusive marriage I had been in for many years. The cycle of abuse breeds secrecy, isolation, denial, embarrassment, and, oddly, the hope that things will change. You get in the habit of making excuses and hanging on, pretending it's not as bad as it is. In my case, it was so extreme that I was threatened with harm, and even death, if I revealed the truth. When I would try to reach out and get help, we'd move to a new location and therefore contact with family and friends decreased until there was none.

Despite these factors, finally, I came alive deep inside. I stopped pretending and thinking things would change. I ceased giving my fears energy and took back power over them, even if just enough to be able to make the break and find the courage to conquer the unknown that lay ahead. I stopped using the excuse, "I'll stay together for the kids," and I became determined to risk setting myself free.

Part of what created this shift was secretly sharing a very minimal glimpse into my world with a long-lost friend whom I reconnected with by chance. She very boldly told me, "René, do you hear yourself? You are being abused, you need to get out!" It was like something snapped in me—someone finally heard and believed me. Together, we plotted my escape.

Yes, I knew I was being abused, but my ex-husband was very deceitful and able to manipulate others into looking the other way, or saying that he wouldn't do it again or that it never happened. After a while, you feel like you are banging your head against a wall, that maybe you're crazy and it's not really as bad as you're making it (though the District Attorney later said it was one of the worst cases he'd seen and that I was lucky to be alive). You feel incapable of finding the emotional courage to rally and reach out for help again, let alone face the possible consequences.

In order to take this big risk to change, I chose to move to a town where I knew no one and didn't even have a job. In one weekend, I packed up a moving truck, drove four hours, hunted for an apartment, sold a car, and used the money to pay for the first and last months' rent on a two-bedroom apartment, leaving me only enough for a few basic essentials. I spent the next week arranging for daycare and school for my daughters, while trying to secure a job to support us. I was scared, I was lonely, and I frequently talked to myself.

Back then, abuse was still a taboo subject not easily discussed, and resources for its survivors not easily found. In the beginning, I really didn't have anyone except myself whom I could rely on or who could guide me forward toward a new horizon.

I realize now I had a purpose to fulfill, though it wasn't exactly clear to me what that purpose was at the time. It wasn't inspired and blissful. I even recall throwing my hands up a few times, calling out to the universe, "Enough already...I've proven I am strong!" Nevertheless, something inside of me didn't give up and kept me going, pushing me past my boundaries.

Though I thought I was only acting out of a survival instinct then, I eventually recognized that I'd had to find the courage, planning, focus, and unrelenting spirit to move to a strange town, go through the transformation and the extensive, grueling legal process, and start a new life. Years later, I realized what a significant defining moment it was in my life.

Every time I stepped *into* fear and *away* from comfort, I grew, I learned something new about myself, I adapted, and I expressed my potential more completely. Embracing and viewing risks as opportunities to grow were critical to my journey, and they will be to yours, too.

Let me share three actual client stories and the benefits of facing risks to change and leave your comfort zone.

Client 1: Not taking risks was influencing her beliefs and her ability to make decisions that would create something new for herself. She kept recreating what she had and wondered why it didn't change. She finally realized that she could only rise to her own expectations, and if those were low or the same as today, she couldn't change. In addition, she was lacking a selfhonoring approach in the way she allowed herself to be treated in her relationships at work and with her family. She had "taught" others how to treat her, and it reinforced her negative, restrictive beliefs about herself.

By choosing to change, she realized what was holding her back and that she could change for the better. Many avenues started opening up in her life. It became easier to stand up for her ideas and herself. It became easier to show up as herself. Interestingly, she also shared how others commented that she had changed, how she even looked younger, less stressed and happier. People couldn't put their finger on what was different. She knew it was because with her new confidence she was growing, was becoming more relaxed, and moved through changes more easily.

Client 2: She didn't take risks to grow for fear that if she did, and changed into the powerful self she was craving to become, she wouldn't still be accepted, liked by others, and even loved by her family. So, rather than risk losing that acceptance, she lived for years in the role in which everyone knew her. Inside she was miserable, tolerating her existence, which made her defensive, angry, and lonely because she wasn't allowing herself to connect differently with others for fear they'd see her flaws. Her self-care suffered and she lacked integration with her life's purpose. Outside, she was successful in her career and was the delightful host who tried to fill her loneliness with lots of parties. She planned her time and needs around everyone else, and this left her short on fulfilling her own needs.

In applying this principle of taking risks, she was able to improve the setting of boundaries by respecting herself and her time. She learned to communicate her needs confidently and asked for the support to change and grow. She dispelled the assumption that she wouldn't still be loved or accepted. She was able to be true to herself, lessen her anxiety, and increase her joy and personal fulfillment.

Client 3: Taking risks on the outside was easy to do. She was adventurous in sporting activities, loved a challenge, and many people liked her. She had her own small business that was doing okay, but she struggled with getting her team to grow and stretch toward the larger goals. She ended up picking up much of the slack, which then cut into her family time and created resentment. When she came to me, she wasn't happy at her current level and didn't understand why she couldn't seem to grow her business or motivate her team to be leaders. She discovered that she secretly feared success and how she might handle it once she achieved it. Hence, she was keeping herself from it, not believing she was worthy or capable of success, which resulted in not communicating her vision confidently to her team.

This third client's personal story is not the first one I've come across that shows an ability to take risks on the outside but not on the inside. These women battled against themselves. They engaged in self-sabotaging behaviors to keep themselves from rising to the next level of success. They actually ran from their success rather than toward it, which took so much more time and emotional energy than creating a plan they could believe in and building trust in themselves that they would make the right decisions and not lose their authenticity to the success they could create.

Instead, this client became self-empowered. She learned to take the responsibility and the risks necessary to change her thinking and behavior. In the end, she embraced her personal greatness and looked forward to the vision of success she aspired to.

See risk as your ally

In this Power Zone Principle, I am not referring to the conventional notion of risk, such as evaluating a common business risk. I am, however, encouraging you to look at risk differently, as an opportunity to shift your thinking and behavioral styles to stretch out of your comfort zone.

Taking risks can be more like a wonderful journey you are about to embark upon—one filled with possibilities. I'm sure there were things in the past you've risked doing, like trying a new activity that created fun or feelings of joy you couldn't have imagined.

Instead of seeing risk as a hurdle, a mountain to climb or a barrier to your success, I invite you to look at risk as your ally. Be willing to be honest with yourself and let yourself fully benefit in this process. Taking a risk is a chance to build trust in yourself and allow yourself to show up and passionately claim WHO you really are.

The strategy to tap into this Power Zone Principle is:

Identify at least one way of thinking, or one thought, and its resulting behavior, that you could benefit from changing in order to begin stretching toward your vision of success. You'll use the chart on the following page to work through this and determine a new behavior you can commit to.

Here are some questions to get you started:

- What is standing between you and unfulfilled possibilities?

- What changes do you need to make to start living your vision of success today?
- What do you need to do, that isn't being done, to lead you closer to this accomplishment?
- What could make the biggest difference between where you are now and where you want to be?
- What will it take for you to step out of your comfort zone?
- Where are the boundaries of your comfort zone now?
- How could you expand those boundaries by taking a risk?
- How could you most powerfully impact your life, career or your business right now?

Think big here; don't get stuck in the details of how you'll do it. The power zone principle in the next chapter will provide a structure for that. For now, just focus on defining the ways you might step out of your comfort zone.

You'll know when you've found them because you'll feel it in your belly – nervousness, fear, excitement – maybe your head will even be spinning a bit. It's that "sense of knowing" feeling. It may even be the one you felt when something stirred inside to get you to start this journey with me.

You might want to run in the other direction or get into a debate with yourself about why none of this is possible.

But the more resistance you're feeling, the closer you probably are to identifying the most important risk you need to take right now. Remember, there is a difference between being content and feeling rewarded by your efforts versus being scared, feeling lazy, or unfulfilled.

What risks do you need to take in order to fulfill your vision of success statement? What restrictive thinking is creating unhealthy habits and behaviors? What key actions can you take to transform your life?

My Thinking	My resulting behaviour	How does it make me feel?	What am I willing to do differently?

Wrapping up:

Eventually, you will have to face the areas you want to change, whether it happens one year, five years or ten years from now. Putting on blinders will not make this necessity go away. It's not going to disappear or dissolve by itself. Nobody else is going to address it — you have to do it. Ask yourself, when is enough, enough? Stop working from a place of conflict. Set yourself free and make the choice to use your personal power and create the change you desire.

Let go of your guilt, claim your story and prepare to write a new one. Shift from feeling it's not possible to change or go after what you really want, to excitement in the journey that lies ahead of you. Work to build trust in yourself and realize that you are more than today's limitations and boundaries.

Become a leader in your life and challenge yourself to overcome obstacle thinking and you'll position yourself for opportunities to take risks to grow beyond your wildest imagination! Let go of emotional hang-ups; don't hold back because you think you lack the skills, and let go of the belief that you are not good or deserving enough. If you have a hard time wrapping yourself around this, take the focus off of yourself; instead, think in terms of who is in need of my gifts, who can heal from them or get inspired, and what do I need to do to serve these people.

Your personal greatness is calling you, will you answer?

Using the Six Power Zone Principles™, you can overcome the challenges to take each of the risks you identified in the exercise. The secret is to work on them one at a time, minimize that feeling of being overwhelmed and maximize success! By doing so, you can take consistent steps forward while sustaining your gains and building your confidence to take further steps.

Leading your life from your power zone takes less mental energy than staying in your comfort zone! Moreover, when you live life from the power zone, your mental and physical energy is naturally working at a higher wattage. It's like turning up the light in a dim room. Things become brighter and more natural energy flows through the room.

You'll hear me say this over and over: your personal power is always there, it's only diminished by your own self-doubt. Turn up the wattage!!

"We are all such a waste of our potential, like three-way lamps using one-way bulbs."   —*Mignon McLaughlin*

Chapter Three

Power Zone Principle #3

Create a Focus Action Plan

"Ninety-eight percent of people in the world are drifting through life with no plan or purpose. This is the major cause of failure. Greatness comes to those who develop a burning desire to achieve high goals."

—*Napoleon Hill*

Creating Your Focus Action Plan

"Motivation is when your dreams put on work clothes."

—*Parkes Robinson*

Having defined your vision of success and identified essential risks, where do you go from here? It's time to get to work! In this chapter, you'll learn how to create a Focus Action Plan to establish your goals and target your vision of success.

The principle and benefits of setting goals have been around for a long time, and there are many methods to structure a goal. For the most part, a common objective is to determine if the goal is worthwhile to obtain, clarify specifically what you want to achieve and then determine the action steps to get you there. I find it fascinating that even with documented evidence on the importance of goal setting, this fundamental principle is either missed or we fail to embrace it. I see this take place not only in personal lives but in established businesses too.

Typically, I find that women don't realize that a plan with supporting goals is necessary outside of their business or work. Unfortunately, this is why many are stuck in their current situation, wondering if it's ever going to get better.

It's amazing how the majority of people make more detailed plans for a trip to the movies than they ever make about their larger future. Think about it: you plan the time, location, what you'll wear, whether you'll buy snacks, if you'll take the kids or get a sitter and so forth. In contrast, how much detail goes into planning for who you want to become and what you want to achieve in your life? When is the last time you set and achieved a goal for yourself?

Why so much attention to focus?

I call my goal-setting process a Focus Action Plan, because it is not enough to create the plan—it must become a key focus to draw out the right actions in order for you to be successful. Therefore, it must be a top priority, and though many things are pulling you in different directions, your plan needs regular attention.

I strongly suggest these plans should be in writing and not kept in your head or only to yourself. In fact, getting ideas out of your head allows you to improve upon them, communicate them to others and refer to them often to confirm you're on target. The plan should focus on priorities, and should have enough details to clearly delineate the goals, action strategies, and the tactics you'll use to achieve them. Ideally, it should motivate you into action, while creating strategic focus. There should also be clear, tangible measurements of success, with larger benchmarks broken into smaller ones to work toward.

---

it is not enough to create the plan—it must become a key focus to draw out the right actions...

All too often I've seen that without clearly-structured goals that support a plan of action, there can be unnecessary struggles, decreased confidence, a sense of failure, missed opportunities, miscommunications, unmet expectations, and damaged relationships.

Furthermore, you may also experience a loss of time and money from reactive behaviors that result in putting out fires, or a starting-and-stopping pattern from lack of planning. You may end up working harder than you need to and often on the wrong things. The list goes on and on.

Here are a few benefits or learning opportunities that my clients have shared:

"Having clear goals makes me feel less overwhelmed, and it feels more tangible."

"I am less stressed when I plan out, what's in my head on paper, and then improving upon what is in my head with the process."

"I can see how long it will really take and feel less stress to get it done."

"I worry less, and [setting goals] makes it easier to evaluate my needs and wants."

"I can see quicker if I am really committed to it or not."

"I am no longer white-knuckling it. I have belief and confidence in myself."

"Having a plan allows for reassessing, and with discoveries made, I can adjust action steps and build my confidence to pace myself so I can follow through."

"The greatest benefit, even better than getting organized, is the power of choice, the feeling of being in control and the belief I can decide where I want to take my future." (one of my favorites)

How I became clear on the importance of a Focus Action Plan

I have lectured and conducted seminars on this topic many times, and authored an international continuing education course about it. I have evaluated personal goals and business plans, launched national projects, problem solved, outlined job descriptions and project plans, and so much more, all using this important component. I share my own benefits of the process because I am passionate that creating a Focus Action Plan is a <u>must have</u> and a <u>must master</u> principle if you want to lead your life from the power zone and, ultimately, in the direction of your vision of success. However, like most of my clients, I wasn't always this clearly focused.

In the late 1990's, working as a consultant, I was traveling and my flight was delayed. I wandered into the airport bookstore with the intention to buy a magazine to take my mind off all the work ahead. I felt I was making good progress with my clients and had many ideas in place. While browsing through the books, I came across Aim First! by Lee T. Silber. As I thumbed through it, my responsive and driven side took over as I recognized the many pearls of wisdom inside, and I purchased the book.

Its pages contained a wealth of information on the power of goals. As an added bonus, I discovered the inside cover had been personally signed by Lee himself and read, *"Have the courage to go for your goals and great things will happen."* It spoke to me.

The message of this tiny book inspired me to assess what I had achieved so far with the skills and methods I was using and begin to think of what else I might be able to achieve or become if I was even more strategic. I became hungry for additional knowledge and excited about learning and sharing it with my clients. Like others, I hadn't fully understood the power of writing down specific and measurable goals, so I began to read other books. I learned about other factors that shaped my beliefs, such as the importance of not working on peripheral goals that only chip away at the problems and generally consume so much more time and money. Knowing how to identify the key areas to focus on will not only produce quicker results, but it will make things less complicated and so much more rewarding.

What's the big deal with a Focus Action Plan?

It's interesting how we'd never think to get in our cars and drive to another state, or even another city, without using a map. Yet, we often set out on personal explorations without a clear plan. Then we wind up wondering how we got so far off course, or why we even thought about taking on the challenge in the first place. This can make us feel lost and frustrated and cause us to give up a perfectly good idea. Alternatively, we might even keep going in the same direction, looking for signs to turn and hoping to get on the right road to reach our intended destination.

I've found that although we might write down thoughts about our vision, such as ideas or dreams, we don't dot the i's, cross the t's, or look ahead at how this will truly impact us. We also don't consider the resources or support we'll need to accomplish our vision.

In order to fulfill your Vision of Success, you'll need to construct a plan and have the confidence to adhere to it, which you'll have if you set down a written course of action, a "road map" of how you'll get there.

Why this matters:

- It is the rare client, after years of experience, who has been able to set goals and make them happen without writing them down first. But even these talented women recognize the many benefits of this step, such as an increased accountability and focus when they do apply it.

• If you are an avid goal setter, you can benefit from finetuning and challenging yourself to evaluate whether or not you are getting all you can out of your goals.

• If you shy away from creating a plan, usually because either you don't know how, don't understand its importance, or you fear the commitment to follow through that written goals create, this will be another growing opportunity for you.

Overall, with this Power Zone Principle, you'll be able to accurately assess if your goal is realistic or not. You can mitigate your risks by identifying in advance the obstacles you may face, and building solutions into your plan using your strengths and resources. As a result, you'll be able to shape your decision-making process because you'll remain proactive rather than reactive by using the plan. As an added benefit, you'll lessen stress and increase your motivation to see it through.

With all you may have on your plate, it can be tempting to skip this step, but I want to say it one more time and be very clear. You WILL miss the benefit: the power of focus and increased confidence in your ability to manifest your vision. I even sweeten the pot by encouraging you to give yourself a reward for the exciting results you can obtain. Yes, that is one of the steps. Everyone likes rewards!

Consider this familiar reason why goals fail:

One common reason why goals usually fail is due to a condition I call January-itis. Have you ever been to the gym in January and there isn't a single piece of equipment available, but if you wait until, say, mid-February, you'll have your favorite treadmill back? Why? This is because of the "all or nothing" scenario created by the belief that just because we want it, we should be able to get it TODAY. Wrong. This attitude will set you up for failure and definitely lowers your confidence level, making it harder to try again.

While enthusiasm is an essential ingredient to successfully achieving your goals, you must have the other ingredient— a plan clearly detailing the steps and measurements of progress—or your enthusiasm will be short lived and you will not follow through.

To prevent this scenario, make sure that your plan encompasses the following steps.

While enthusiasm is an essential ingredient...you must have the other ingredient—a plan.

Getting Started – The Focus Action Plan (FAP)

Start by choosing where to put your focus. Do this by using either the most essential risk you deemed necessary to take in order to change your thinking or behaviors, or, pick one of these key elements (value, service, special, true goal) from your Vision of Success statement. You'll want to work on either an internal or external goal depending on what you discovered about yourself in the previous sections and what will make the biggest difference to help you begin taking steps to lead your life from your power zone.

The risk or vision element you choose to work on will become your first priority to create your Focus Action Plan (FAP). You will be able to choose another one and use this process repeatedly. So, start with just one to build your goal-setting muscles.

Step 1: My Priority (Goal)

Something to Consider:

If the priority you selected is easy or won't take much effort, it probably will not make an impact on your vision of success.

In this process, you are working to take powerful, lifetransforming steps that will allow you to boldly leave your comfort zone. A good indicator of whether it will make an impact is the energy attached to it.

How easy does this goal seem to you? Does it require you to take risks to grow? Have you found the one that will make the biggest difference in shifting your course? Ask yourself and evaluate the best place to focus your energy.

This is *your* journey, and *you* will ultimately decide where to put your mark. Work to strengthen your ability to use your personal greatness and increase belief in yourself by powerfully choosing where to put your focus.

Step 2: Identify your current situation.

Using a scale of 1-10 (1=lowest, 10=highest), rate where you are today in relation to achieving this goal (e.g., 1-=a thought, 8=almost there).

Circle your current rating: **1 2 3 4 5 6 7 8 9 10**

Describe what this rating looks like in its current state. What are you doing or not doing? What challenges do you face? Get specific, so that you know where you are now and can easily measure your progress.

_____

_____

_____

_____

Step 3: Identify your desired results.

Using the same scale of 1-10, rate where you want to grow toward in the next <u>30 to 90</u> days. Keep in mind that in this timeframe you'll want to increase by no more than 1 to 3 steps from your current rating. Circle the desired rating you want to target for your goal: **1 2 3 4 5 6 7 8 9 10**

Describe what makes this rating different than your current one. Don't detail what a level 10 would look like. Here you want to focus on the rating increase, what you are doing now, and what you will have achieved. Be specific so you know exactly what you are working toward and can easily set specific action steps.

_____

_____

_____

_____

Note: You may want to target your entire vision of success and tackle all the thinking and behaviors you want to change. However, resist the temptation to try to take them on all at once or in short periods of time. If you feel up to it, you can look a year ahead and then back yourself down into 90-day increments to get you there.

Depending on your priority/goal and the desired results, there can be several mini goals that break down the steps even further inside an overall larger goal. For example, a goal that will take several months can be broken into smaller steps to enable you to start today.

Why not just go for the 10?

Think of yourself standing at the starting point and in one giant leap, you have to cover 10 steps. Could you do it? Probably not. You might end up doing the splits, with your legs stretched uncomfortably and painfully apart, and there's a definite possibility you'll land right on your behind or have a serious injury.

Either way, you'll need to take time to re-adjust and build up your courage all over again before attempting another step.

No matter what number you are starting from, taking smaller, consistent steps, one at a time, will strengthen your legs so when you get to 10, you can stand and <u>maintain</u> your gains and be positioned to take the next step confidently. Pace yourself and enjoy the process. This is a marathon, not a sprint!

Fact: You simply can't complete a 10-step goal in a single bound!

Next, in the FAP process, use the SMART Goal questionnaire to detail the Action Steps to achieve the "Desired Result" you described.

The SMART Goal Questions:

(SMART is an acronym widely used, this is my rendition of it.)

Specific—Measurable—Achievable—Reasonable—Timed

Step 4: Identify the specific details necessary to accurately target your goals.

This is probably one of the most important steps, but it is the most often neglected. The success of your plan hinges on this step. Why? We often believe that, just because we want something, we'll know what to do to get it without missing a step. This is a risky assumption. While it may be easy to take action on your day-to-day tasks or agendas, targeting your big goals or taking actions to stretch toward your Vision of Success, especially if you want to be successful and enjoy the journey, will require more planning on your part.

The key in this step is to refer to your desired results and take time to identify each specific "action step" you'll need to include to make this happen. If you leave it too broad, then you can't accurately target the steps. You must look at how long your steps may take, what order you need to do them in, what resources you might need, and if there are scheduling or support considerations. The effort you take here will save you not only time and resources but the possible frustration in getting down the path and revealing all the should-haves, could-haves, wish-I-would've-known's that your plan lacks.

Specific

What specifically are you referring to? What is the first step, the second and so forth? Avoid broad statements; create detailed specific action steps so you can measure if you are on track and can easily correct your course if you aren't.

Step 5: Use this step to keep your enthusiasm high and increase your ability to keep your commitments through clear measurements of success.

The outer measurement is the tangible sum of the results you'll get after pursuing all the specific action steps you have outlined. When you complete this part, it should agree with your desired results and give an overall point you can target, i.e., "I created ... I completed ... I now have ..., etc." What would be the biggest impact in achieving your goal?

The inner measurement starts with realizing that we are emotional human beings. We aim for the inner emotional measurements of satisfaction just as much, if not more so, than the outside physical results. This is represented in how you feel such as "I feel calmer and more peaceful," "I feel courageous, passionate and confident," or, "I feel aligned with my power zone." Whatever your measurement is, you should be able to identify with it and know if you have been successful by how you feel.

In fact, if you meet these outer results but don't sense a measure of success, whatever it may be, you'll end up feeling let down, resentful of all the work you did, and may even jump on another goal—maybe not the right one—while still trying to reach that failed inner measurement. Be aware that you are also seeking the emotional fulfillment this goal will bring. Make sure you know what that is.

Here are some additional questions to ask yourself to draw out the inner/outer measurements: How do you know when you've arrived at your desired place? How do you know if you're getting close, if you're going off course, or even if you're getting distracted?

It's like driving. You want to keep your hands on the wheel and be able to see clearly if you start to drift into another lane or if there is an obstacle in front of you. Being able to see clearly will help you keep your motivation high and increase your momentum to see the path through. Seeing signs of progress is like enjoying the wind in your sails. It keeps pushing you toward the horizon!

Measurable

How will you know you are successful? There are two measurements to consider here. The Outer: What will success look like? The Inner: How will that make me feel? These will act as your personal GPS system, telling you if you are on course and keep you from second-guessing yourself.

Outer: _____

_____

Inner: _____

_____

Step 6: Use this step so you don't end up stuck or off course.

Not completing this step is why you'll sometimes end up stuck or off course when you thought your goal was achievable.

I find that often, as busy professional women, because we are already good at multi-tasking, we can be guilty of the "I can do anything if I just do it" syndrome. However, this can create overwhelming pressure to rely on the idea that there will be a way to just squeeze it in. If you fall into this trap it will set you up to fail. Don't consider what you can do to cram it in, but rather to honor the time you have allotted (30 to 90 days) in which you can accomplish each step and stay motivated. Besides assessing the timing, also consider if you have what you need to carry it through to successful completion. Remember this is meant to help you grow, so including areas for improvement into your action steps, like learning a new skill, is perfectly fine. Careful thought here on what it will take to achieve each action step will help you build a sound plan.

When you are done, check again with your specific and measurement steps and make any adjustments before you proceed. Any goal is achievable, so long as it is realistic and you are willing to break it into smaller steps, making it achievable one step at a time.

Achievable

Is your action step achievable, yes or no? If the answer is yes, note why, and move to the next question. If it is no, go back and be more specific about the action steps until this priority is realistically achievable. Consider whether your specific action steps have enough details to make them achievable. An example of this would be: Yes, this is detailed enough so I can begin to take steps to make this happen. Or No, I need to ask more questions, get more details, or break it down into smaller steps so I can begin.

_____

_____

_____

_____

Step 7: Use this step to ensure you'll have the support and resources necessary to see the goal through.

This step helps to identify any outside resources or other people's support you'll need to secure. By not identifying these in advance, actions may be stalled and follow through hindered. Take time now to address these and determine what needs to be included in the specifics of your goal.

You can do this by determining if there is anyone you need to talk to before completing your plan. Ask them what they need to complete their part and include time for their portion and any research you might need to do. This includes support from family (including your spouse), vendors or your team, basically anyone besides you who has a part in the success of your desired results. If it is reasonable, you won't feel overwhelmed and won't be relying so heavily on others. It will be a balanced approach and a collaborative process. If it isn't reasonable, that doesn't necessarily mean you can't still achieve your goal; the goal may just be too big for the allotted time period. Evaluate and design a reasonable goal. Avoid all-ornothing thinking and work toward progress.

Reasonable

How reasonable is it to achieve your plan at this time? Consider current situations and possible support or resources you might need. If it doesn't feel reasonable, then your goal may be too large. You might write something like: Yes, I don't have any limitations to overcome so I can achieve this now. If No, go back and determine ways to make it reasonable and include these in the specific step, then check in with the measurements and achievable steps again to make any adjustments.

_____

_____

_____

_____

Step 8: Use this step to reduce feeling overwhelmed.

List the date(s) you wish to commit to completing the action step(s) of the SMART goal you've outlined here. All the steps should be completed within the 30 to 90 day timeframe.

If your goal is specific enough, you should be able to start taking steps within a short period of time, say a week or two. You can break the action steps down by weeks, calendar dates or milestones.

Establishing realistic timelines can dramatically reduce the feeling of being overwhelmed. At this point, you should be excited, and I am confident that if you follow this process you will have a solid goal to target.

Enthusiasm is important, but in doing everything you can to keep highly energized to reach your most gratifying goals, the danger is that you may drive yourself too hard. I also know from personal experience that it is easy to take on too much and feel less than successful. This can create doubt and frustration. Consider the natural ebb and flow of your life and use this in the timing of your plans. Employ flexibility here, especially if you are relying on others or have others depending on you.

Remember, this is a journey to success, and you are working to create progress and personal transformation. Build on this first step, then choose another goal and arrive at the next level of success until eventually you attain your whole vision.

Timed Action Steps

What specifically are you going to do, and in what timeframe?

The result you want is to create realistic, measurable action steps that can be undertaken within a short period of time (30 to 90 days). Ideally, your progress should be made each week until the goal or priority is met. This, in turn, will build confidence, which is needed to stay consistent and follow through. If you cannot take steps within a short period, go back and get more specific until you can do so within your means. Larger goals are not achieved in one leap but rather through consistent smaller steps that propel you toward the final desired result.

_____

_____

_____

_____

Note: What if I can't assign a completion date to my goal, or it's something ongoing I need to work on? Some goals will not have a calendar date you can easily attach to them; i.e., "I want to stop my negative thinking that creates an unhealthy behavior." These types of goals may be ongoing and are not reached and completed by a set date, yet they can be quantified in this process by answering the questions. If you get specific as to what is happening today pursuant to your thinking and behavior, then you should be able to identify specific areas in which you want to see improvement. Those desired improvements can then be given a by-when date, and using the measurement step, you can indicate what differences you should notice, i.e., "I would have this thought or behavior only one time a week versus every day." This process works for other progressive, ongoing goals as well.

Now that you have completed the SMART Goal questions, you are ready to finish the (FAP) process–continue with the next step.

Step 9: Use this step to set you up for success.

Did you get everything covered? Have you taken advantage of your talents and gifts to achieve this goal? Have you thought of outside strengths that you can leverage? It's like packing your suitcase for a trip. Did you pack everything you need? Do you have all your essentials so you can close your suitcase and feel secure you have everything? Go ahead and make any fine-tuning adjustments at this time. Even take a day or two to think about it, or run it by someone you trust who can be objective. You want to feel like you have work to do, but it should feel attainable, and you should feel confident in your plan.

Obstacles—These *"could"* prevent the achievement of your goal. These may be either internal and/or external. The word *"could"* is emphasized because the obstacles may merely be based on perception. By dealing with them in advance, they can be overcome.

Examples of obstacles:

Internal—Negative self-beliefs, fear of failure, or the lack of desire or willingness to see the steps through.

External—Agreement and support from team members (spouse, family, friends) may be necessary.

Strengths can help overcome the obstacles and reinforce goal attainment. These, too, can be both internal and external.

Examples of strengths:

Internal—High self-esteem, positive beliefs based on past achievements.

External—Others' willingness to support the goal or methods to implement change.

Once you have evaluated strengths and obstacles, review your previous SMART goal steps. Check to see if these present additional factors that need to be considered when defining your goal. If so, go back to the Specific step and include those details. Then go on to the Measurable step, and continue. If you build ways to overcome obstacles and increase strengths in pursuit of your goals, they will be easier to attain.

Strengths & Obstacles

"If there are no obstacles between you and your goal, it is probably not a goal at all, merely an activity."

—Bryan Tracy

What strengths do you have that you can tap into to get the desired outcome? What obstacles do you need to overcome using your strengths?

_____

_____

_____

_____

Step 10: The fastest way to increase energy, motivation and follow through is by celebrating your successes.

This step is typically one of the hardest to commit to at first. You wouldn't think so, as everyone likes rewards, right? Honestly, think about it: when was the last time you gave yourself a reward for achieving your goals? At first it can seem awkward, and often my new clients view a successful result as reward enough. While there certainly is reward in getting to the finish line, that is not the same as acknowledging a job well done and savoring all you have done to get there. Not only is celebrating success your right, but self-acknowledgment and validation are important to building confidence and increasing your willingness to take new risks to continue to grow. We'll address this point further in Principle #4.

What is success, what is failure and what does each mean to you? Do you define it or do you allow others to define it for you? Sometimes, you may have done all you can but didn't achieve all you wanted. If you have a plan, and you've worked at it and have done your best, who is to say you failed? Things out of your control may happen so be open and be patient with yourself.

A reward can take many shapes. Be sure to invite others, such as your support team and family, to celebrate with you. During your goal attainment process, use your journal to document your thoughts and ideas and make affirmations. If things get tough and you start to doubt, you can look back and remind yourself why you want this and what you hope to gain from seeing it through. Whether it is for a smaller goal or for benchmarks during a lengthy goal. Creating rewards is a great motivator. "What gets rewarded gets done!"

Rewards

How will you reward yourself when you achieve your goal? What will you do to celebrate your success?

A clearly-defined goal will naturally increase motivation to go further because it looks and feels tangible. However, motivation can quickly fade if measurable, consistent progress is not acknowledged or rewarded. This is particularly true if you are working to change long-standing habits or are taking bold steps out of your comfort zone. Rewards will help you want to stay the course.

_____

_____

_____

_____

"More important than talent, strength, or knowledge is the ability to set goals and enjoy the pursuit of those goals. My advice is whatever your goals, don't ever give up."

– Amy Grant

Tips to stay motivated and increase follow-through:

- Realize you cannot do it overnight - it is a process.
- Break larger goals into smaller goals.
- Be open to shortcuts or better ways to do things. • Cross off your goals when you accomplish them.
- Assign a reward when benchmarks are achieved.
- Get support from others and share your progress.
- Be flexible and willing to reassess, and even rewrite, your goals.
- Use visual aids to motivate you, like pictures and positive quotes.
- Avoid "all-or-nothing" thinking; get started one small step at a time.
- Allow enough time, be patient, and build in flexibility.
- Take time to assess the goal, determine whether you are on track, and make changes as needed.

Your life is "dynamic," and sometimes things will come up that require reassessing your goals to determine where you should go from here. Focus on the positive. Don't panic; see it as a challenge and build it into your plan. Then keep going!

Symptoms of not applying this principle:

- You will wonder if you are working on the right things that will make the biggest difference.
- You may feel disjointed, overwhelmed, and not in control of your life.
- You will lack confidence and believability to lead your life from your power zone.
- You will act small in your life and may not stretch to become the woman you can.
- You will not be able to overcome challenges and obstacles from a proactive position.
- You will continue to follow the path of least resistance.
- You will feel afraid to share your goals and be accountable.

Benefits from applying this principle:

- You'll improve your ability to create focus and take bold steps toward your passions and purpose.
- You'll have higher self-confidence, resulting in increased happiness and success.
- You'll start to see other opportunities and smarter ways to get ahead.
- Your enthusiasm to take risks toward growth will increase.
- You'll spend your time working on the right things and get more done than you ever thought possible.
- Your mental energy and sense of personal fulfillment will greatly improve.
- You will recognize accomplishments by celebrating your successes.
- You will begin living in your Vision of Success!

FAP Overview:

Step 1: Choose one priority to focus on; this is the first goal you'll create using the Focus Action Plan process.

Step 2: Be clear on what your current situation looks like.

Step 3: Detail what will be different when you reach your desired results.

Step 4: Break your desired results into specific action steps that allow you to begin taking action right away.

Step 5: Establish inside and outside measurements of success.

Step 6: Determine if your plan is achievable, considering timing, realistic steps and any skills you may need.

Step 7: Determine if your plan is reasonable, considering support and resources you may need.

Step 8: Assign completion dates to each action step, resulting in an overall date of 30-90 days.

Step 9: Identify your obstacles and resolve them in advance by making sure you have assessed how you can use your strengths.

Step 10: Set a reward and celebrate your success when you achieve your goal.

As you can see, these are not difficult steps — they are just steps. If you take the time to do them, you will create strategic focus and increase your motivating energy. This, in turn, will enable you to move forward toward your vision of success one step at a time.

Wrapping up:

Your personal greatness is calling you and you CAN answer! Manageable steps will help you set your goals in motion, build trust in yourself, sustain your personal commitments through motivation and accountability. All this while you take intelligent risks to stretch out of your comfort zone and into your power zone.

Written goals take the guesswork out of how you will successfully arrive at your desired destination. Like any other important plan, review it often, acknowledging progress and checking off what has been achieved. Be open to reassessing and establishing new timelines and specific steps as needed.

Goal setting is an ongoing process. Once you achieve your goals, it is important to reassess the new situation and set new goals to maintain the results or to grow to the next level of happiness and success.

"Occasionally dreams come true, but not as often as goals do."
—*Unknown*

The strategies you will learn about in the next chapter will help to build your confidence so that you can stay true to your Vision of Success when creating and implementing your Focus Action Plan.

Chapter Four

Power Zone Principle #4

Overcome The Four Confidence Blockers

"With realization of one's own potential and self-confidence in one's ability, one can build a better world."

—Dalai Lama

Overcoming The Confidence Blockers

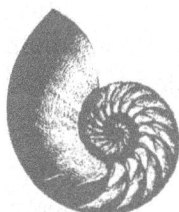

"How often in life we complete a task that was beyond the capability of the person we were when we started it."

—*Robert Brault*

The first three Power Zone Principles are extremely important, but we really can't proceed any further until we address this important issue. Confidence Blockers are insidious success barriers that control the decisions you make and the way you react to various situations.

The strategies we'll discuss in this chapter—identifying and overcoming your fears, removing internal barriers and unleashing your assertiveness and commitment to self-care— all work together to build your confidence and help you overcome the Four Confidence Blockers:

Fears

Internal Barriers

Lack of Assertiveness

Lack of Self-Care

How do these affect you?

A confident woman is someone who is in touch with her personal power zone and is able to champion her fears and use them as growth opportunities. She understands the influence of her self talk and beliefs, and demonstrates this through her assertiveness to take risks and show up, and who knows she is deserving of self-care.

When a woman is not expressing her full level of confidence, she is not in tune with, or may have forgotten, the power she possesses. Because of this, her fears manifest themselves and influence her actions, thus suppressing her growth and validating her negative self talk and harmful beliefs that, in turn, fuel more fears. A fearful woman is much less likely to assert herself and take risks, and may feel unworthy to take care of herself. Not applying the four strategies works against her, inhibiting her confidence and preventing her from leaving her comfort zone.

Confidence Blockers hinder your ability to take the risks necessary for true success in your life.

Confidence Blockers hinder your ability to take the risks necessary for true success in your life. All too often I see that, if unchecked and left to their own devices, they take on a life of their own, resulting in a retreat to your comfort zone, where negative self-talk can thrive and where there's no risk-taking and, as a result, no progress.

The strategies in the next section will help you to overcome your Confidence Blockers and will further enable you to take necessary steps to move forward to the next level of success in your professional or personal goals.

Understanding the importance of how these strategies can unfold in your life will help you "play bigger," instead of "staying small." Paying regular attention to these blockers and taking steps to eliminate them will lessen your stress and make it easier to stay on course. Take a deep breath, find your courage and face these once and for all. If you don't, I guarantee these will keep you from accessing your personal strengths, your positive beliefs and your core driving energy, all of which are found in your power zone.

The bottom line: if left unresolved, these blockers will keep you from accessing your powerful self. Everything you want lies just outside of your comfort zone. You deserve more, so accept the challenge and welcome the changes ahead.

The CRES System

We'll begin addressing the confidence blockers by introducing you to my CRES System: (Confidence and Risk Emerging Strategies™) in the next four sections.

After years of working with individuals and organizations, I discovered I was continually addressing common challenges not easily recognizable by the client at first, and so I created this system to tackle the four confidence blockers I typically found holding them back from achieving their goals and dreams.

The CRES System is an important part of the Six Power Zone Principles™ and was designed to help professional women increase self awareness, and thereby increase their potential to be passionately empowered leaders in their lives and work. By doing so, they are enabled to achieve their next level of success. The system in this chapter is made up of understanding the Four Confidence Blockers, your CRES Score, the strategies to overcome your blockers and the

CRES Worksheet — all designed to give you a method to practice integrating Power Zone Principle #4 into your life.

The purpose is to challenge women to recognize the areas in which they are limiting themselves, and then provide a process to stretch their comfort zones to increase their confidence, their personal power, and to take risks to help them grow. From my professional experience I know that when self-

confidence is high, there is a shift in the energy devoted to any task, which increases a woman's personal desire to claim her greatness and ultimately fulfill her vision of success.

Self-confidence is arguably one of the most important traits you can have because it influences all areas of your life. Selfconfidence shows up in your actions, speech and demeanor. It's an outward reflection of the way you feel about yourself on the inside. Self-confidence plays a crucial part in determining your happiness and success throughout your life

Let's start with the first step. On the next page, you'll work on your CRES Score. Take a moment now to complete the selfevaluation. If you want a general overview, I suggest you consider your responses for how you have felt or what you have thought in the past 30 days; for a more focused result, consider the past 7 days.

As you progress through the next four sections, you'll have the chance to use the CRES Worksheet to assess and track your progress in overcoming your confidence blockers as you go after your goals by setting up action steps and rating your results.

What's Your CRES Score?

Begin by finding out your CRES Score. On a scale of **1 to 10**, rate how often you say or think the following statements:

10 = never (or not applicable), **5** = sometimes (once a week), **1** = once a day (or more)

1. _____I'm afraid of moving to the next level – what if I fail? What if I succeed?
2. _____I worry about what other people are thinking of me.
3. _____I just don't know if I can do this.
4. _____I need approval from someone else in order to trust my own ideas.
5. _____I find it difficult to enjoy family time without worrying about work and vice versa.
6. _____I wish I could stop procrastinating (avoiding starting or finishing projects)!
7. _____I know where I want to get to, but I don't know where to start.
8. _____I start on things but never seem to follow-through.
9. _____I just don't know where the time goes.
10. _____My big goals seem to have gotten lost among daily responsibilities.
11. _____My team members (or support team) don't understand what I'm telling them.
12. _____I'm too tired to work.
13. _____I just can't concentrate.
14. _____I feel so stressed out.
15. _____I feel so down, I wonder if all this work is worth it.
16. _____I know that my health and well-being need more attention.

Give yourself a score for each strategy by adding up your points for specific questions. A <u>low score</u> indicates that this be a good area for you to focus on as you continue through this book.

To determine your score for <u>Strategy One,</u> Identify and Overcoming your Fears, add up your scores from questions 1, 2 and 6, and see what your total is out of 30. 30 is your highest possible score and 3 is your lowest possible score.

To determine your score for <u>Strategy Two,</u> Remove Internal Barriers, add up your scores from questions 3, 4 and 5, and see what your total is out of 30. 30 is your highest possible score and 3 is your lowest possible score.

To determine your score for <u>Strategy Three,</u> Unleash Your Assertiveness, add up your scores from questions 6 (again), 7, 8, 9, 10 and 11, and see what your total is out of 60. 60 is your highest possibly score and 6 is your lowest possible score.

To determine your score for <u>Strategy Four,</u> Commit to SelfCare, add up your scores from questions 12, 13, 14, 15 and 16 and see what your total is out of 50. 50 is your highest possible score and 5 is your lowest possible score.

My CRES Score shows I could benefit from raising my CRES score, especially for strategy number _____

I agree with this because:

_____

_____

Strategy One: Identify and Overcome Your Fears

> *"You gain strength, courage and confidence by every experience in which you really stop to look fear in the face. You must do the thing you think you cannot do."*
> —*Eleanor Roosevelt*

The "Stuff" that Fear is Made of

Recognizing that we have a fear can be a new and challenging task, but it is an essential part of the confidence-building system. Once we have the courage to name a fear, we can look more closely at it to see whether it's rational or irrational.

By naming your fear and evaluating whether it's rational or irrational, you can take back the power that your fear has taken from you. A good place to start is to get the fear out of your head and onto paper, where you can actually see it for what it is and do something with it, instead of letting it spread out of control.

Fear is a protective mechanism our body uses to keep us from harm. In everyday life there are going to be problems that we have to face and solve that may not be necessarily harmful. These may include unpleasant events, financial worries, job loss, stressful relationships and so forth; even if we fear them and really just wish we could avoid them, we will need to address them at some point.

If your fear is *rational*, ask yourself, "What's the worst thing that could happen if that were to come true?" or, "What would I do if that happened?" That will start to diffuse the negative energy around the fear and get you in a proactive position so you can use the Focus Action Plan principle to help you design and implement a solution.

A rational fear is based on a real experience, has evidence, and is not based solely on emotions. However, each time you find the courage to face your rational fears head on you'll reinforce the knowledge that, no matter what happens, you can bounce back and continue moving forward. Too much energy goes into avoidance and denial when you ignore your rational fears. Keep in mind that's a temporary solution at best. This type of fear and the problematic situation created by it, has a tendency to get bigger and become more challenging to unravel. Try to break it down into smaller more manageable steps, or just dig in and resolve it as best you can.

On the other hand, our *irrational* fears are made up of four elements that may be present separately or combined – assumptions, interpretations, gremlins and outer challenges.

Assumptions

An assumption fear is based on something that you perceive happened in the past or a belief that something is true even without proof. Based on your perception of the experience, you presume it will happen again.

How to recognize when assumptions are present:

You might think to yourself, "Why bother? It's just going to happen again." Or you might presume that you can read someone's mind and predict their response to your work, words, or actions. You may take things for granted by judging a situation or person without recognizing that things can change; your judgment is clouded by what you perceive happened in the past.

When it comes to going after your goals, you might be hesitant to try if you've had an experience that didn't give you the results you wanted. Your assumptions lead to fear and paralysis; you want to stay away from whatever experiences have "burned" you in the past.

When your fear is fueled by an assumption:

Really pay attention to your thoughts and find the assumption that may be underlying them. Think back to the original situation or other experiences that have led you to make that assumption. And then ask yourself, "What if that wasn't really true?" If you still feel it was true, ask yourself, "Is it useful today?"

Then go further and ask, "What is another possibility?" or "Could there be another reason?" and "What do I want to do with it today?"

You have the power to create your own truth and to act as if the world is with you instead of against you. That kind of positive thinking will draw positive results. However, you have to be open to looking at things differently to create new perceptions, empowering thoughts, and positive assumptions.

The next step is to create a new message by writing it out and reading it often, This will help test your new, positive assumption – the one you created specifically to help you shift from the old one. So, whatever accomplishment you've been avoiding because of an assumption-based fear is now in your power to achieve!

Interpretations

Your "reality" is a story that's being told inside of your head, based on your previous experiences and your current state of mind. Yet, to you, right now, it feels like the absolute truth.

How to recognize when interpretations are present:

You may play this "story" out in your head with every detail before it even takes place. I find this happens particularly with women. We have worry down to an art form. We will imagine all the details, conversations and even have the conclusion already mapped out. Most often, this scenario, or soap opera, doesn't take place, and we have wasted so much emotional energy on it. And while we did this, we missed out on being truly present in our life because we are on guard, looking for ways to validate this fear and, as a result, we are often in a reactive mode.

Another clue is that others may have a very different view of events. You may have a hard time seeing from another's perspective. You may not recognize that a fear is irrational and not based on actual reality (but on your own brand of reality).

When your fear is fueled by interpretations:

Put it in writing. Be brief and as factual and "non-emotional" as you can. Try stepping back and act as if you are an outsider viewing it for the first time. What do you see? Write that down. Catch yourself if you find yourself agreeing strongly with your previous notes and push to see it from another perspective. Act as a detective and ask yourself, "What else could this mean?" then "If I had to give a different argument for this what would I say?" Now you have another way of looking at it and another way to act.

Consider this common scenario. Most likely, you have had a girlfriend, a sister, or another woman call you up and tell you their emotionally-charged interpretation of an event or something that was said. You can't get a word in edgewise since they see it in such black-and-white terms. You, on the other hand, are not emotionally connected and can easily see that there is probably another way to interpret this drama. We can see other perspectives for someone else's concerns, but it's harder to do this for ourselves. However, if you learn to step back and check if there's another way to view a specific circumstance, this will save you so much emotional turmoil. You always have the power to choose how you will react and where you'll give your precious time and energy. When you are in touch with your power zone you will see your world in a whole new way.

Gremlins

The "Gremlin" is a coaching term for an embodiment of a self-belief that was created in the past. It is made up of deeprooted fears and negative personal messages about ourselves, ones we have worked hard to reinforce and hold on to.

How to recognize that your Gremlin is present:

The Gremlin is that part of you that "talks" to you in "I" statements—"I am not good enough"; "I am not capable"; or "I'll never get this right." It is very emotionally charged and takes the power away from you.

The Gremlin diminishes your confidence for the sole purpose of reinforcing your past belief. When you begin to grow or change, the Gremlin feels threatened. It's sneaky, working to keep you in the "comfort zone" believing things are just the way they should be (i.e. the way they always have been), instead of embracing the risks and changes that are needed to move you forward.

When your fear is fueled by your Gremlin:

Begin by acknowledging its existence and give it permission to come out in the open. Have compassion for your Gremlin. It's that internal part of you that is very uncomfortable with change, feels vulnerable and even scared and is just trying to love and protect you by keeping you in your comfort zone. This is a myth, since it's not working for you but is instead causing unhealthy habits and behaviors while it saps your personal power and greatness. This part of you wants you to stay where you are now because, although it doesn't really work, it's used to handling it.

Anywhere you go from here involves a risk that where you end up might not be as comfortable. Change isn't always comfortable at first, but in order to fulfill your vision of success you'll need to shift and grow. That's a big trigger for your Gremlin.

Here is an exercise you can do to get in touch with this part of you and start to talk to yourself from your powerful side. Close your eyes and try to picture your Gremlin – your image of your internal fear. Visualize what it looks like. Be quiet, calm your mind and listen for it. Notice what it sounds like when it speaks to you. Listen to the words and messages it is telling you. Let it speak out until it feels heard.

Next, have a conversation with it. Though it may feel awkward at first, with practice my clients have found that they can clearly see and hear their Gremlin, which can come in any shape, size, and color. This is a very liberating and empowering exercise, if you'll allow yourself to explore it.

Once you are in touch with your Gremlin, ask questions such as, "Why are you here today?" or, "What are you trying to protect me from?" Listen to your deep inner self. Don't argue or justify, but let it all come out so you can see clearly what your Gremlin is made of, or how it was created. This can bring up strong emotions including guilt and sadness. Be kind to yourself and don't judge or be hard on yourself. Remember you are working to release and shift to a life lived inside your power zone. On the other side of those recently released emotions is joy, love, peace and abundance all waiting for you to embrace them.

When you're ready, thank the Gremlin for trying to protect you. Then ask it to use its desire to support you in another way: use its energy to help you be confident to overcome the fear. You can even give it a new name to help you both (logical and emotional sides) remember that it now has a new job. This also becomes a positive word to use whenever you hear the negative "I am" messages. You can say the new name, like Eagle, Champion, or Peace, and trigger the awareness to remember you don't have to go there so you can shift your thoughts in a more loving and self-honoring direction.

It will take practice but soon you'll recognize which side of you is talking and quickly shift to your powerful self. Your Gremlin-based fear can have a big hold on you. When you release that hold you'll be rewarded with access to all of the energy that was previously tied up in protecting you from change.

Outer Challenges

Sometimes our fear of action is based on outside circumstances that we feel unable to control or fully understand. We feel these are blocking us from achieving our goal. Some of our fears related to outer challenges are irrational and some are rational, as we addressed at the beginning of this section.

How to recognize when outer challenges are present:

You may feel frustrated and hopeless, like you're beating your head against a wall or like you're a victim of circumstance. It's really important to distinguish between the outer challenges you CAN control and the ones you CAN'T.

When you're holding back from taking action because your mind is fixated on an outer challenge you can't control, that's irrational and ineffective.

However, when your fear is fueled by an outer challenge you CAN control, it's actually a very rational fear and one you can do something about.

For instance, the new promotion you want may involve some job skills that you don't have. You could hope and wish that were different (focusing on the part of the situation that you can't control). You could also feel like you're being discriminated against because you don't have those skills (not particularly constructive thinking), or you could take the action to get yourself the training and practice to develop those skills (focusing on the part of the situation that you can control).

When your fear is fueled by outer challenges:

Make a list of the outer challenges associated with your fear and identify the ones that you can change. Compile a list of solutions and suggestions, no matter how far-fetched or unrealistic they may seem. You can even use a method for creative problem solving or a brainstorming technique to let your creativity and ideas flow freely. What's important is to get them out of your head and down on paper so you can see what you have control over.

Next, take a look at your ideas and group like ones together until you start to see a pattern or a formal plan emerge. Run your ideas through the FAP questions and set a realistic goal you can achieve. Make sure to determine what kind of support you may need from others, including advice or solutions.

Keep in mind, being a confident woman <u>doesn't mean you have all the answers</u>. It means you're secure enough to seek out the people, resources and solutions you need to overcome obstacles and challenges. It means that you invite the support of others, listen thoughtfully and with an open mind, and then determine whether or not that advice will help you to fulfill your vision of success. We'll go into more detail on this in a later chapter, but for now, be open to other possibilities.

Wrapping up:

Dealing with fear is really about first recognizing it and then claiming your power to choose how to handle the situation that you're fearful of. Choose not to give away your power or control but instead to trust yourself to deal with the unknown. When you are leading your life from the power zone, you will have a higher level of trust and believability in yourself. You will look at things differently and notice more quickly if your fears are rational or irrational.

When you can identify, understand and then release your fears, the energy that was blocking you is now accessible to help you. With fear, energy goes inward and is closed down inside you, preventing you from taking action or being open to taking advantage of opportunities.

When fear is released, that energy goes outward and you access your place of confidence so that you become a more powerful conduit for that newly shifted energy.

As a result, you're more able and willing to claim your fears and any unhealthy habits or behaviors. Remember, even successful women have fears. Don't put your blinders on; rather, recognize the symptoms, commit to change and undertake them one at a time.

The qualities you will develop by applying this strategy are:

Risk-taking—Resilience—Persistence—Flexibility

The challenges you will overcome from the CRES Score are:

- The fear of failure, fear of success ("I'm afraid of moving to the next level – what if I fail? What if I succeed?")

- Procrastination ("I procrastinate by avoiding starting or finishing projects")
- People-pleasing ("I worry about what other people are thinking of me")

Using The CRES Worksheet every week, you'll have the opportunity to address a new fear (or continue to work on an existing fear that's stubborn) by creating an action step that will help you overcome it.

Let's start right now by identifying your first confidence blocker — the irrational fear that's blocking the confidence to achieve your Vision of Success and supporting goals.

My irrational fear is:

_____

Now, go through the explanations of assumptions, interpretations, gremlins and outer challenges, and write down which one you think is fueling your fear:

My fear is being fueled by:

_____

Now, select one of the suggestions shared in this strategy that will help you deal with that fear:

You'll fill this "Action Step" into the first row of your CRES Worksheet located at the back of this chapter.

"Become so wrapped up in something that you forget to be afraid."

—Lady Bird Johnson

Strategy Two: Remove Internal Barriers

"They can because they think they can." —*Virgil*

The Internal Success Barriers

Do you ever spend time daydreaming, letting your imagination run away with you? Do you ever daydream about your next level of success? What does it look like? What do you feel like when you're imagining that you're there?

When you daydream, you're accessing your right brain, which is the creative and feminine side of your personality.

Daydreams are often viewed as light-hearted, silly fantasies or wishful thinking, and they can be. But actually, many athletes, musicians and business leaders rely on positive daydreaming (visualizing a positive outcome to an upcoming event) to achieve success.

Research has shown that when these elite performers spend time visualizing that perfect jump, closing that high-power deal, or hitting that home run, they have a better chance of actually making it happen.

Daydreaming, however, can be a harmful practice when you're spending that time ruminating on what went wrong or what could go wrong. When you worry, you are visualizing an unwanted or negative outcome to a situation. By repeating these negative images in your mind, you are more likely to make them happen.

Daydreaming is just one example of how our thoughts are processed throughout the day. Sometimes they're positive, motivating and encouraging and sometimes they're negative, worrisome and harmful.

There are three types of internal success barriers blocking you from positive thinking and keeping you working from a negative perspective – limiting beliefs, thought stopping, and internal messages. In order to reach your goal and fulfill your vision of success, you need to be able to identify and understand these.

Limiting Beliefs

Do you believe you can have what you want? Do you believe you deserve to have it? If you don't, chances are you're harboring some limiting beliefs. Until you can turn those around, you'll keep bumping against them and they'll block your path to success.

Limiting beliefs are thoughts and opinions that we've learned along the way and have come to accept as truth. They generally come from external information. They are considered limiting as they inhibit our perceptions of what we'll be able to do, who we can become, or what we can achieve.

How to recognize when limiting beliefs are present:

Limiting beliefs are being expressed when you have thoughts like:

- Women can never reach the same level of respect and success in business as men.
- I have to take care of everyone else before I do anything for myself.
- It takes struggling, sacrifice, hard work, and long hours to become successful.
- Success takes luck and I just don't have it.
- I have to be a certain weight and height to be beautiful.
- Acknowledging my successes would be bragging.

When limiting beliefs are holding you back:

You have the power to choose what you believe. Your experience in life and work is a product of your belief system.

I'm sure you know the phrase "seeing is believing." By believing and having gratitude for your successes, you can visualize your future. Doing so can keep you positive and encouraged as you take purposeful actions from your Focus Action Plan.

Our thoughts are very powerful. We can make our own realities, our own fate and our own luck. By focusing our energy and thoughts on what we want, we can offset our own negative thinking. That is how powerful we are!

Contrary to what you may think, making your Vision of Success come true won't be because of hard work and unrelenting focus. Instead, it will take imagination, belief and a higher expectation of yourself FIRST, and then you'll be inspired into action to manifest your dreams. Understanding this point, and having a clear vision and a plan to get there, can help you bridge the gap between thinking about and living out your dreams.

Here are some techniques to dispel limiting beliefs and bring future dreams into the present:

~*Affirmations*: I used to take this one lightly until I was challenged by my coach years ago to manifest what I desire. I now know firsthand how this works; this book is proof of that. If you are not accustomed to doing this, as I wasn't, write out some of the positive messages in this book and post them on your bathroom mirror. Then read them out loud every morning until you get in touch with and believe in your powerful self. There are guidelines and examples later in this chapter. One that I used early on was simply, "I am deserving." I remember reading this until I felt calm, present, and open to attract the success I desired for the day.

~An illustrated goal or picture frame: We think in pictures, not words. Use a large photo album to start collecting pictures that remind you of your dreams. Put one of your favorite images into a frame and display it. Create a poster board and cut out pictures of what your vision looks like. See it as if it were already here, get excited, and create a desire for it. By doing so, your willingness to do what is necessary to achieve it or become it will naturally increase and you won't be filled with limiting beliefs; instead you will manifest your goals.

~An ideas book: Have you ever come up with a great idea when you're in bed, in the shower, or driving? Keep a notebook handy to capture those gems before you lose them. Over the years, I have benefited from jotting down quick idea generators or "aha" moments. My favorites are ones with open, undefined space. I am more structure-oriented in nature so using an idea book, like a journal, also serves to allow me to practice just letting any idea go where it pleases. I find it liberating and energizing, recognizing that some of my best ideas have come by doing this. You also might capture an idea that could be your greatest one yet.

~Checklist: Check off small steps as you achieve them and remember to reward yourself. It is through the small steps that you will reach your goals and have the confidence and energy to sustain them. On the professional side — crossing off your to-do list allows you to acknowledge all you are doing, to prioritize, and see where you are going so you can pace yourself. This is a great way to dispel negative beliefs about your abilities. It's hard to argue with yourself when you can see all the check marks. On the personal side — My oldest daughter has taken after me and is a list tyrant. In November 2007, she visited for my wedding, and as we

prepared, she carried her todo list everywhere she went. As a result, the wedding came off perfectly and most importantly, I remembered my luggage. Unfortunately, my husband, who now thanks me for my listmaking, planning side, left his behind. I tried not to tease him too much.

~*Journal*: Document your thoughts and feelings about the benefits you'll receive as you achieve your goals. Use your journal to champion your fears as you challenge yourself to attain your goals and visualize your true self and the world around you. Hear your internal chatter and practice not judging yourself. Work on overcoming limiting beliefs by committing to one week of writing down your thoughts, daily activities, fears, and hopes. Don't read it; just record your thoughts during the day including what you did, how you felt, your successes, your challenges, dreams, etc. After the week, read your entire week's worth of entries, and from an outside perspective, acknowledge what comes forth on the pages. You'll see your internal messages, beliefs, how you view yourself, personal judgments and your capabilities very clearly. You'll see opportunities for improvement that you might not have seen otherwise. Determine what you want to work on first in the coming week and set a plan to do it. It's tempting to resist this exercise because it's new and frightening because of the personal truths you might discover. But soon you'll see the benefits of taking just 10-15 minutes each day to get present in your life. The result is you'll own who you are and move to your powerful self and start leading your life from the power zone.

~*Positive daydreaming*: Spend five minutes each day visualizing your success in detail. Use your Vision of Success. The first thing in the morning is the best time for this as it will help you set the tone for the day and get in touch with the positive feelings. It will also raise your desire and willingness to be selfaccountable to the goals and desires in your vision.

Thought Stopping

These are thoughts that can "stop" your growth or prevent you from moving forward or taking essential risks. These mirror some of the strategies I've shared, but this is another internal barrier we need to overcome. These are crucial, and your participation in these steps can only work to your benefit.

Our thoughts control us. Can we control them? Thoughts are our inside talk. Negative thoughts bring negative outcomes. Conversely, positive thoughts bring positive outcomes. The choice is ours.

Our emotions, our personal energy, our actions, and the resulting outcomes are all directly influenced by our inside talk. The core messages from our thoughts are present every moment of every day whether we are aware of them or not.

We use our core messages for simple tasks like deciding where to go for lunch or what movie to watch. We tap into them for life choices such as deciding to accept a promotion, start a family, or buy a house. We rely on them to protect us and keep us from danger.

Those internal thoughts enable us to do extraordinary things. But the amazing power of our thoughts is largely untapped, on automatic pilot, for the most part. It is only when we choose to make a conscious effort to put our hands on the wheel and take charge that we can change our thoughts and our course for the better.

Why should we put energy into paying attention to our thoughts when so much is already going on automatically? That's just it. We often live on autopilot and all have things we "should do" according to our personal beliefs. "Should do" thoughts don't generate much positive energy and often lead to procrastination.

However, our inside talk, our thoughts, can increase our desire and energy just as much as negative talk takes it away!

How to recognize when thought stopping is present:

When your energy is feeling stagnant, stuck or blocked, you can suspect that there is some thought stopping going on.

There is limited access to your energy in this state and your inner source of power is unavailable to you.

If this happens, you'll feel stalled and will have less desire to take action. You might procrastinate and make excuses.

When thought stopping is stopping YOU:

Change your thoughts to ones that work for you. Look at the phrases in the column on the left and for the next week practice recognizing when these appear and reframe it by replacing it with the empowering thoughts in the column on the right.

When you think:	Change it to:
I should	I prefer to
I ought to	I desire to
I have to	I choose to
I must	I want to
I'll try	I am

If you have a regular thought stopping word, you can pick just one to practice each day for a week. Write it down and with the replacement word, and post it where you'll see it several times each day, like your desk, car visor, day planner or bathroom mirror. Start shifting your thoughts as soon as you sense the emergence of negative or limiting ones. Feel the energy difference from just saying the two sets of words. Notice that one is more motivating, with forward energy that puts you in the driver's seat, whereas the other sounds stalled, held back, drained of energy and doesn't make you feel as powerful.

You will be amazed to see how you really think and the untapped power you'll release. Remember, the real power of personal transformation lies in the small steps you'll take to change. The rewards of doing so will be great.

Internal Messages

We are what we think we are. Our internal self-talk creates a message proclaiming who we believe we are. We all have a general message of how we feel about ourselves and our own personal truths. There have been many reports and studies in the recent years demonstrating that our actions, or lack of action, are influenced by what we think about ourselves and what we believe to be true for us.

How to recognize when negative internal messages are present:

Internal messages show up in our choices and how we speak about our capabilities or feel about ourselves. They can be mixed with fears and limiting beliefs.

Ideas to create new positive messages:

"Re-framing" negative self-talk is crucial to a different outcome. You can re-learn how to talk to yourself so that the old messages are replaced.

One structured form of positive self-talk is called "affirmation," as addressed earlier. An affirmation statement is a positive phrase that acknowledges something as if it is already happening. It is affirming the future you want while still in the present.

Affirmation statements help eliminate:

- Negative beliefs you have about yourself
- Self-deprecating statements that you make about yourself in everyday conversation
- Negative thoughts that influence your behavior

Here are some guidelines for creating an affirmation statement:

Put your affirmation statement in writing. It can be one sentence or an entire declaration.

Use powerful, positive language in the present tense, i.e. I am, I will, I can, or I believe.

Here are some examples of affirmation statements:

I AM - I am in control. I am strong. I am taking one step at a time and will allow my life to be everything I deserve.

I AM - I am able to handle any problem I face. I am successful and I deserve more success. I am a capable, intelligent, loving woman.

I WILL - I will face my fears courageously. I will challenge myself to step out of my comfort zone. I will take a risk to grow today.

I CAN - I can manage my time more effectively. I can increase my confidence. I can be assertive. I can take risks. I can let go of fear.

I BELIEVE - I believe, allow, and trust in my life purpose.

Practice in your journal to create new, positive messages and use it to track your negative thoughts. The better you become at noticing your negative thoughts, the better you'll be able to practice and then master replacing them with positive ones.

Ensure that your environment is conducive for positive thinking. Negative people and clutter are two examples of things in your environment that may be contributing to your negative internal messages.

The different types of internal barriers that we've discussed are depleting your energy, power, and confidence. When you can identify and understand your internal barriers and take action to free yourself from them, you can replenish that source of power, increase your level of desire and get motivated into action.

Our thoughts come with a warranty, yes, a warranty. If you don't like the ones you have, you can replace them with more positive and useful ones.

When you shift your thoughts, you'll shift your focus and the thrust of your energy. This reframing of your thoughts will help you to see things differently and will empower you to be more positive and proactive about what is happening in your life. This allows you to shift to a desired action and outcome, focusing on the positive experiences or feelings you get from doing so.

Like anything new, it takes effort to make changes and create new habits. Be patient with yourself and start small by simply paying close attention to your thoughts and how they propel you forward toward your vision of success and goals, or if they're stopping you from this progress.

When you shift your thoughts, you'll shift your focus and the thrust of your energy.

Consider the external influences that affect your thoughts and reactions. Creating awareness is powerful and allows you the opportunity to prevent being controlled so you can be proactive instead.

Remember, you always have the power of choice. What is happening may not be your preference, but your reaction to it and the influence it can have on your thoughts and your life is ALWAYS YOURS!

The qualities you will develop by addressing these internal barriers are:

Risk-taking—Creativity—Self-reliance—Intuition

The challenges you will overcome from the CRES Score are:

- Self-doubt ("I just don't know if I can do this")

- Need for external validation ("I need approval from someone else in order to trust my own ideas")

- Guilt and worry when you're not focused on family and/ or business ("I find it difficult to enjoy family time without worrying about work, and vice versa")

Using The CRES Worksheet, you'll have the opportunity to address a new internal barrier (or continue to work on an existing one that you haven't been able to address) by creating an action step that will help you overcome it. To overcome this second type of confidence blocker, begin by writing out the top four negative or self-limiting thoughts that are standing in your way.

1. _____

2. _____

3. _____

4. _____

Now, determine which of the above internal barriers are creating these thoughts and choose one of the suggested action steps in this section that will help you to remove it. This is the "Action Step" for the second row of your CRES Worksheet at the back of this chapter.

Strategy Three: Unleash Your Assertiveness

> *"People waste more time waiting for someone to take charge of their lives than they do in any other pursuit. Time is life. Time is all there is."* —Gloria Steinem

Drive or be Driven!

Through strategies one and two we've dealt with your inner world. As you're making these huge shifts in addressing your fears and internal barriers, you also need to shift how you interact with the outer world.

You can choose to resign yourself to being a passenger in your life or you can get in the driver's seat and sit squarely with your hands firmly on the wheel. In essence, you can drive or be driven! Which will you choose?

Through assertive self-expression, confidence can grow and you'll be more likely to stay tapped into your power zone. You have a choice to continue the way things are and hope they get better, or to do something about changing them.

You can achieve the things you want when you choose to live your life consciously, setting intentions based on your values. Instead of acting out of default reactions or habit, you can decide where and how to spend your precious energy.

When you consciously lead your life from the power zone, choosing where to spend your energy, you'll naturally distribute your time and talents differently, creating a sense of balance that leaves you feeling more alive and powerful, making your energy count!

It takes time, commitment, courage and focus to unleash your assertiveness, fulfill your vision of success, and move forward to the next level. In this section we'll address ways to unleash your assertiveness through time management, learning to say no, courageous conversations and pursuing your true goals.

Time Management

Typically, I see my clients measure their time management skills based on how busy they are. When greeted and asked how they are, women will generally say they are busy, as a measurement of how they are personally feeling. There is a mentality that "we must always be busy" to be successful and naturally our worth is shown in our level of activity. Not necessarily. Focusing on the right things and being busy are two different things. Yet we typically measure our successful time management by how busy we are.

However, there is another time measurement that is more important and has more influence on what we can actually achieve: our self-worth. Confident women with a high level of self-worth take control of their time, make conscious decisions about how they use it, and set clear boundaries around how other people use it.

This "self-honoring" approach to time management requires tapping into your personal power and confidence, so that you are more willing to take control of the outcome, set boundaries, have the ability to handle challenges gracefully, and enjoy the journey towards your vision of success. This doesn't mean you are being selfish and not willing to serve others, just that you have stopped piecing yourself out so there's not enough of you to go around. Others will appreciate this, because you'll be more pleasant to be around, feel less resentful, and will stop making commitments you can't keep. No more need to apologize when you can't keep them.

How to recognize when time management is a challenge for you:

- Evaluate your schedule. Does it feel like it is running you or are you running it?

- Do fears of success (how you might handle it once you've achieved it) or failure (what if you don't make it?) prevent you from taking control of the time in your day?

- Does stepping out of your comfort zone to experiment with a new routine make you nervous?

- Are you too busy to stop and plan your day?

- Do your to-do lists get longer?

- Is there never enough time to take care of your important tasks?

- Do you feel unfulfilled or unsuccessful at the end of your day?

Ideas for a self-honoring approach to time management:

~*Identify time-wasters and energy-drainers*: You'll know what they are by the way they keep hanging around in your schedule, on your sticky notes and on your to-do list, and how you get that yucky feeling when you see them.

When we procrastinate we sap our energy and consume more time than we realize. When you're stuck, instead of moving forward, the mental and emotional energy you need to stay focused gets stuck inside, as well.

When a task has been incomplete for a while, take a close, honest look at the value of completing it. Then decide to do it or take it off your list.

If you've decided to do it, try using a support person to help you follow through or create accountability for yourself by asking a friend or family member to check in with you about it at a certain time. For the things you want to do, create a hierarchal list of priorities so that the things most important to you get more of your time and attention.

If you decide not to do a task, let it go and enjoy the time and space to apply your powerful energy to something else you truly want to do.

The 4 Step: Decision Making Matrix:

Here's a great way to begin organizing and prioritizing tasks that are taking up your time, and identifying the truly urgent ones from the energy drainers you should let go of. You'll be amazed at the time you'll have left over and how much energy you'll have for the things important to you.

Dump It (1)	Delegate It (2)
Ask yourself, "Will this task get me closer to my vision of success?" If not, dump it! If not today, then set a "dump date" and stick to it. Learn to say, "no, thank you" before the wrong things get onto your list in the first place.	Ask yourself, "Do I need to do this task?" or, "Is this the best use of my time?" If not, then identify who else could do this and then hand it off. Let go of any guilt and regret and focus your energy on doing the right things.
Defer It (3)	**Do It (4)**
Ask yourself, "Does this need to be done immediately?" If not, schedule a specific time at a later date to do it. Keep in mind that certain tasks will benefit from regular, ongoing attention. Deferring them will only cause an overwhelming pile up later on. Set weekly or monthly dedicated times to work through the project piece by piece to stay on top of it.	If you answered, "YES" to the questions, "Will this task get me closer to my vision of success?", "Do I need to do this task?" and, "Does this task need to be done immediately?" then do it now. You have identified an important task that needs your immediate attention. Don't make excuses or fall under the spell of "all-or-nothing thinking" that results in procrastination. Break the task into smaller steps and reward yourself often.

Look at your schedule for one day and use the number next to each decision to rate the type of activities you find on your calendar. Put a number next to each appointment or task, based on the descriptions. What do you see? How many of each do you have? Where should you take action first? Are you sure you are the only one who can do this? What should you delegate—even if only a portion? What should come off your calendar? What should you defer today so you can handle your do-its and instead set up a regular time to create focus on them each day, week, or month?

I have a system that allows my clients to use this decisionmaking process to create a road map to arrange their day for success, to organize emails, file folders and in boxes and much more. This allows them to get back into the driver's seat and deal with what they have control over.

There are many benefits from analyzing and organizing your time. You'll feel in control again and less anxious, able to make decisions easier, celebrate more successes, and enjoy your days more because you aren't taking the all-or-nothing approach. Realize that you don't need to do everything. Restore your balance and allow yourself to get in touch with your power zone and ignite enthusiasm and desire to keep approaching your time and life in a self-honoring way.

Setting daily intentions:

Setting daily intentions is about taking responsibility and control for the daily actions that YOU can and will complete by aligning your attitude, beliefs and actions to them. This is a key ingredient in staying connected with your larger vision of success and to keep your believability and confidence high.

This is a key point. The most important thoughts of the day are at the beginning of the day. They set the tone and set you up for success. Days are always more focused, purposeful, and successful when you utilize this process.

Things can really change for the better once you learn to master the art of setting daily intentions. You become very clear about what you want in your life and work, and what you need to do each day to achieve it. You become better at prioritizing and setting boundaries.

Without a clear road map or idea of how you are going to get there, you will likely end up somewhere else. You'll work harder. You get more stressed. Your quality of work will decline. This causes more stress, which means you have to work more hours, thus causing your work to slide even further into the abyss. It's a vicious cycle!

Take responsibility and control of your actions to create your desired outcome and this will help you live a life of intention versus a life of default. When making your goals, include setting your intentions for each day, week, month and year, and then COMMIT to those intentions. Again, keep these aligned with your Focus Action Plan and they will naturally support your vision of success. Setting intentions helps you keep a daily perspective of the bigger picture.

The steps to set your intentions:

Take 15-30 minutes each morning to quietly **reflect** on your daily goals, **review** your plans for achieving them, and **consider** any adjustments or improvements to that plan. **Refer** to your posted Vision of Success Statement. You can also keep a copy of your statement in your planner. **Evaluate** whether or not the activities or tasks planned will get you closer to your vision of success or not.

Measure a day's success by the quality of work you accomplished, not the quantity. Ask yourself, "What would today look like if I was successful?" How would I feel? Does your day allow you to achieve this or not? Will you end up at the end of the day feeling your measurement of success? If not, ask yourself, "What would make the biggest difference today on how I spend my time?" Make adjustments to create your measurement of success. If you have commitments, make a note of them and decide whether, once you complete them, they should end up back in your calendar again.

Aim to let go of less important tasks as a measure of success and focus on the big picture of achieving your vision of success.

Tip: Once you do this, follow through. Be sure you set realistic intentions. Set yourself up for success with smaller steps and then get them done and keep moving forward. Setting your expectations too high can leave you stalled and cause you to slide backwards. As you begin to feel more comfortable with the process, then you can start taking bigger steps and setting larger intentions.

Learning to Say No

Other people make countless demands on our time and energy. But it's not just about learning to say "no" to others; it's about learning NOT to automatically say "yes." **How to recognize when saying no is a problem for you:**

- When you're having trouble saying no, you may feel pressure to please everyone.

- You're resentful that time is being taken away from fulfilling your own dreams and feel guilty when you say yes but don't follow through on your commitments.

- If you find yourself feeling indispensable, it's a good sign that your thinking is distorted and that you're taking responsibility for things that are not your responsibility.

Ideas for saying no:

~*Pause*: You can pause before you answer, or even let them know that you can't answer right now and you'll get back to them. A simple explanation is best, such as, "I need to check on some other commitments and get back to you."

~*Use the Four-Step- Decision Matrix*: Take their request through this (see earlier in this chapter), and then give them an answer.

~*Be gracious*: "Thank you for asking, but I'm unable to help at this time." Resist the temptation to over explain or over promise that you'll be available later.

~*Win/Win*: Help them see that adding their request to your full plate won't provide the results they're looking for. Express your appreciation for asking, but explain that you don't want to compromise the success of their project by taking on something you really don't have time to do your best work on.

~*Allow someone else to grow*: When you resist the urge to fill every request, you give opportunities for others to step into those roles and stretch and grow. Let go of the guilt and allow others to build their skills.

~*Do what guys do*: When a guy says no, he says just that. NO. Okay, he might add "No, dude," or "I can't, man." But he doesn't start into detailed justifications or explanations of why he can't do something until he's eventually convinced to say yes. As women, we need to practice this guilt-free way of saying NO! Last tip here: when you do this, zip your lip and sit on your hands, resist the urge to speak after "No, thank you." Be okay with the silence.

Courageous Conversations

I am a firm believer that you teach people how to treat you! To show up powerfully and confidently in your relationships you must learn to set boundaries and limits, ask for and allow support, be able to let go of past challenges, and ask for and give forgiveness.

How to recognize when courageous conversations might be needed:

- When you're lacking courage in your communication you may find yourself avoiding certain people because you're uncomfortable with something you said, didn't say, wish you'd said, or wish you hadn't said.

- You may wonder why it is people seem to always misunderstand what you were trying to say.

- You may have given up on trying to make these relationships better and now you're tolerating behaviors that you find unacceptable.

- You find that others are frequently making last-minute requests or demands on your time, expecting you to put their needs over yours.

Ideas for how to have courageous conversations:

~Talk to yourself: Step up and out of your comfort zone by having the most important conversation, the one with yourself. Confronting yourself can be intimidating at first. Ask yourself what it costs you to not be direct with yourself. What could you gain and be free of if you did? Take quiet time to reflect. Use a journal to write out your thoughts and connect to your powerful self. Listen to yourself and tap into your wisdom and self-love. Once you can be direct and accepting of yourself it will be easier to be that way with others because you won't be so defensive or put yourself in a position that you can't live up to. You will be able to be more compassionate and help to create shared motivation.

~Let go of the need to be right: Is your viewpoint or need to be right holding you back in relationships? If so, own anything you need to and be open to other viewpoints. You don't have to address them directly to do this since it really is about *your* perception of the situation. You can write a letter to the person or to yourself and release the energy, committing to move on once your letter is done.

~Embrace that life is about learning: You have the right to make mistakes and the right to learn and grow from them. Those life lessons are gifts you learn and you can grow even more so by passing those pearls onto others. Consider how you might turn these into growing opportunities by planning to resolve, accept any consequences and then forgive yourself and move forward. Don't let the energy drain you any more!

~Address the Boundary Breakers: Face your fears of what you think might happen if you speak up and have the conversation with the person or persons you have allowed to disrespect your time and, in essence, you. Notice that, if they are repeat offenders, you have enabled them and taught them that this is acceptable. Come up with a list of reasons describing how you having to drop everything to compensate for their lack of planning doesn't help them or you; nor does it often get the best results or allow you to keep your own commitments. If it's someone at work, you may need to sit down with your boss and get their support. Have the conversation, and stick to it the next time they make a boundary-breaking request. Repeat offenders have bad habits they'll never change if you keep "permitting" them, even if it's "just this one last time."

Going after True "Primary" Goals not Secondary

Many tasks that find their way onto your to-do list keep you plenty busy but don't actually move you forward. They might be somewhat related to your vision of success, but they're not the key actions that will get you there. I refer to these as secondary or peripheral goals and they are different than true goals.

Oftentimes someone else has added these; maybe to that person it's a true goal. Sometimes we added them ourselves, possibly because we got distracted from our vision of success by something that seemed more compelling, interesting, or achievable.

It's essential to stay focused on your true goals. These are the goals that you know "deep inside" that you need to work on, the ones you identified in the Vision of Success exercise. They represent your calling, your life purpose, and what you want to achieve. When in doubt, true goals ignite the spark in your power zone.

How to recognize when secondary goals are distracting you:

- Old tapes, the internal messages of who you can or should be are present and are holding you back.

- You feel like you have to justify your wants and needs.

- You make excuses that now is not the right time and you need to get other things done first.

- You may feel in conflict with your values and how you are living your life.

- You will feel you are not living your purpose or your true measure of success.

Ideas to go after your true goals:

~*Write them down*: Studies have shown you can increase the likelihood of achieving your goals by simply writing them down. (Use the Focus Action Plan principle for this). And you can double your chances by reviewing them often and measuring your progress. Considering that we tend to meet our own expectations (the "self-fulfilling prophecy"), whatever they are, the power of writing out your goals and reviewing them regularly is not to be underestimated. Unleash your assertiveness by claiming what you want through your written commitment and take responsibility for your progress.

~Increase energy and focus: With so many things pulling at us, it's easy to get distracted and off course. Consider using what I call "influencers." These are things you can add to your environment to influence your energy and enhance your ability to create focus. Have you ever heard a certain song come on and noticed an immediate shift in your mood and energy? The task didn't change but your attitude was influenced. Another example is a powerful quote or passage that felt like it was speaking to you, instantly connecting to your true self and inspiring you to take action.   Don't underestimate this power to influence your ability to achieve your true goals.

~Avoid the perfectionist trap: As I have mentioned, from time to time you'll come across internal resistance to achieving your true goals. Be aware that fine-tuning, revising, and continually tinkering with a project can be just another way to avoid completing it or committing to your true goals.

Ways to overcome this are:

1. Commit yourself to the idea that getting the project done (at home or at work) by the designated deadline is your highest priority. You are responsible for it, so stop wasting time and do it.

2. Even if you make an error or it's not perfect, you need to finish it. Make sure you understand the expectations of those who will evaluate your work before you begin.

3. Do your best work and finish by the deadline, but don't defeat yourself with perfectionism. Evaluate what you have done based on the list of expectations, not your own "perceived" ones.

4. Get feedback and allow support so you can stay detached and not connect the results of this project to your own self-worth.

~*Remember the KISS formula*: "Keep It Simple (for) Success! It's the "aha" moments when the smallest changes make the biggest impact. In life and business change is essential, and adaptability to change is vital. Be open to looking for easier ways to get the outcome. It's not how hard you are working, it's whether you are making it harder on yourself by working on the wrong things.

Wrapping up:

Unleashing your assertiveness is one of the biggest challenges women face. They've lived with a tolerance factor so long that they hold themselves back from making their lives easier and more rewarding; as a result, they are not able to work on leaving a legacy behind. They remain great task-doers, not focusing on what they believe in. You have so much more you can achieve.

This is about being fulfilled, living your values and using your gifts in your power zone. It's about speaking up and showing up so you can start taking charge of your life.

Tip: How can you tell the difference between Assertive versus Aggressive? To distinguish between the two consider this. Being assertive is putting forward confidence in your thoughts and ideas, even in the face of adversity. Aggressiveness is putting forth your thoughts and ideas from a confrontational position. When you are assertive, others can see clearly where you stand, and you are open to hear others' opinions or thoughts even if they differ. Aggressiveness gives others the impression that it's wrong or misguided to have an opinion that differs from yours. How can you tell the difference? If you are being aggressive, people will remain silent, not give you feedback or they may want to argue with you. If you are being assertive, you are open to engaging with others who will ask thoughtful questions or challenge you with their ideas, but they are open to input and won't take a combative stance.

Master the foundational principles before you go to the next level. Bigger ideas and strategies do exist. However, without the core foundation you will not be able to support bigger strategies and will end up frustrated and resigned to be a passenger in your life. I challenge you to implement these and see how quickly and confidently you get back in the driver's seat of your life.

The qualities you will develop as you unleash your assertiveness are:

Risk-taking—Assertiveness—Persistence—Resourcefulness

The challenges you will overcome from the CRES Score are:

- Procrastination ("I procrastinate by avoiding starting or finishing projects")
- Not knowing where to start ("I know where I want to get to, but I don't know where to start")
- Poor follow-through ("I start on things but never seem to follow-through")
- Poor time-management ("Some days, I just don't know where the time goes")
- Lack of focus on goals ("My big goals seem to have gotten lost among daily responsibilities")

- Unclear communication ("I don't think I'm being clear and consistent in my communication with team members.")

Using the CRES Worksheet, you'll have the opportunity to practice unleashing your assertiveness. For now, choose the topic from this strategy that you need to work on the most:

- Time management
- Saying no
- Courageous conversations
- Going after your TRUE goals

Now, write an action step from one of my suggestions in that section that will help you to unleash your assertiveness and get past this third type of confidence blocker:

_____

This will go into the "Action Step" in the third row of your CRES Worksheet at the back of this chapter.

Strategy Four: Commit to Self-Care

"You have to fill up yourself so that you have enough to give to others." —Oprah Winfrey

Self-Care for the Mind, Body and Soul

Taking time for self-care seems like a hard thing to do in our busy lives, and there never seems to be enough time. But with practice, establishing small breaks of personal refreshment and then making a commitment to incorporate these into your routine can minimize potentially stressful internal and external barriers and increase your sense of well-being and thus your self-confidence.

It is important on your journey to success to keep your confidence high, as this will directly affect your ability to leave your comfort zone and take the necessary risks to achieve your vision of success. Take time to care for yourself. Feeling run down or unbalanced, having no time to celebrate, and generally feeling depleted of the energy to embrace your purpose will prevent you from tapping into your personal greatness and driving core energy, your power zone, which is necessary to maintain the course on your journey to success.

In this section, you'll learn about reducing stress reactions, work/life balance, celebrating success, and your self-care reservoir.

Reducing Stress Reactions

It's safe to say that all of us want less stress in our lives. While this is a worthwhile goal, I've found that what we really want is less of a "stress reaction" to occurrences in our lives that absorb our energy and personal power. In this section, I make no medical claims but rather my own observations from working with clients. Stress itself is not the biggest problem we face. History shows us we would never have survived as a species if our bodies didn't have the ability to respond to threats.

While we need to be able to react like our ancestors did to potential threats, we have been conditioned to exhibit a "fightor-flight" response to many situations, which may not be appropriate. One effective way to manage stress itself is to learn new skills, such as identifying the sources of your stress and what you do or do not have control over. Next, restructure your priorities and practice a self-honoring approach to time management, and focus on changing your stress reactions.

Stress isn't something we can eliminate, because in our society there are many things that are and always will be stressful. Just watching the evening news can cause stress, and the likelihood of isolating ourselves from hearing about stressful events in the lives of friends and family is not likely to happen. Some stress isn't bad and can create an appropriate sense of urgency, such as meeting a deadline. Don't focus on necessarily removing all stress; rather, pay attention to your reactions as an important part of life management.

How to recognize when stress is causing problems for you:

~What is your body telling you? When you are reacting to stress, you will feel it somewhere in your body.

~You're reacting to external or internal stressors: External stressors are things such as ongoing highly pressured work, long-term relationship problems, or physical conditions such as pain. Internal stressors are things such as work-life balance, personal values not being honored or intense worry about a harmful event that may or may not occur.

~Your energy level is affected: You need to find a proper level that allows you to function. A little healthy pressure to increase productivity is fine but too much zaps your energy, leaves you overwhelmed and unable to focus, encourages procrastination, and can shut you down. This can cause a sort of paralysis, where you freeze up and can't function mentally and emotionally.

~Stories you tell are holding you back: One of the biggest hurdles we as women face is that we let our "stories" get in

the way of doing what we know to do to create the results we want! This causes stress because we are not being true to ourselves. These are stories that act as a defense mechanism, that signal a distress pattern or become a rationalization for doing something that isn't right or doesn't make sense.

Ideas for self-care and reducing stress:

~*Pay attention to your engine warning lights:* If you are like most busy professional women, time seems to run faster than you can, so much so that it sometimes makes your head spin. The option to just stop and catch your breath, regroup, or reprioritize sounds tempting, but perhaps you don't feel like you have time with everything else you need to accomplish.

You figure you might as well just keep at it since more of the same will get you somewhere different, right? Wrong! If you can relate to this: Danger! Your engine warning light is on.

The body's stress response is much like the "engine warning lights" in our cars. Your personal power can start to drain out of you like a car with a bad battery. By all appearances, your car still seems functional. Perhaps it's just a little harder to get things running at full capacity and the lights are starting to dim, but you'll deal with it. Maybe your instrument panel is doing quirky things, but you're still moving.

However, unbeknownst to you, lurking under the hood, your battery is sucking up your energy and your life force. This is equivalent to the demands on your time and your mounting stress from lack of self-care, as your wheels continue to spin.

Okay, don't jump out of the car yet . . . just take hold of the steering wheel of your life! Get proactive again with your choices. See if your tasks and actions align with your goals to determine if your goals are realistic or not.

Let your foot off the gas pedal and pull over for a minute before your engine warning lights come on and you end up calling a tow truck. This may land you in the repair shop for days, which always costs more and takes more time than a quick tune up.

When we learn to pay attention to our bodies, we can see our warning lights telling us that we're in need of maintenance. My warnings show up in my neck and shoulders, telling me that I need to find a better way to manage my stress and take time to release it before I have to stop working because I get a bad headache, which can turn into a migraine, and a whole domino effect is created. A simple 15-minute oil change is easy to do and will get more life out of the engine. The same is true for us. The reverse is also true: the car being in the shop puts us out of commission and creates more stress that could have been prevented.

Tip: Use your intuition and listen to your body; it doesn't lie. Then use your power of choice and make the decision to take care of yourself. Determine in advance, what your "engine warning" lights look like and feel like and a simple step you can take to turn things around at each one. The goal is to catch yourself at the "check oil light" status and have an agreement with yourself of what you'll do to repair it immediately. It's much easier to determine this in advance, as in the warning stages; you may not be able to see opportunities to turn things around later.

A single parent and small business owner commented, "It's amazing how much more 'energy' and clear thinking I have when I schedule breaks in my day."

Sometimes you'll have extensive projects, or "work pushes" as I call them; I had a big one in writing this book. However, I would balance it with time for mental and physical self-care, even just a few minutes snatched here and there helped.

My husband was a big proponent of this. He would even remind me of my own principle, which sometimes annoyed me because I knew he was right. I did appreciate it though, especially since it was good for me. My level of creativity and energy always increased when I did this, making it easier to stay motivated and keep the creative juices flowing. It kept me from feeling overwhelmed which helped me stay excited and keep my perspective on my bigger vision.

~*Changing your stress reactions:* As we noted, there will always be things out of your control, and you will have to face stressors in your life. Everyone has their limit as to how much stress they can handle. Even the most even-tempered people have been known to fly off the handle at times, but this is usually caused from a build up of stress. Decide before things occur how you will handle them. What's your plan and how will you honor yourself in the process? What can you do to release the pressure even in small ways so you don't boil up like a pressure cooker? Losing yourself to stress will not allow you to keep your power and your decision making will be affected, which further takes your power and increases your stress level. Stay as proactive as you can. When you change how you think, your actions will follow.

~*Avoiding freezing up*: If stress is extreme or ongoing over a period of time, it causes what I call a mental freeze, in which the person goes into a hibernation mode, blocking reality and pretending it's not there. This reinforces irrational fears and in worst cases, causes an emotional mental paralysis, which freezes any positive actions necessary to shift the energy. When this happens, let someone you trust support you. Take time to check in with your fears, start to release the tension by finding the one thing you can control, no matter how small, and start to feel your strength again and then move onto the next one. Avoid the all-or-nothing approach, as it will only make things worse.

~*Recognizing your story:* How many of the following stories do you recognize in yourself?

- I want to grow/I feel there is more for me. I wish I knew how to fulfill my potential, so when I figure it out I'll be ready for help.
- I worry I am going to fail so I put off getting started. I just need to spend more time figuring out what I need to do.
- I don't know why I can't seem to stay motivated and follow through, I just need to keep telling myself to do it and get it done.

If even one of these hit home on any level with you, your story (your excuses) could be keeping you in a "holding pattern" and causing a limitation or rationalization that is making your decisions for you. It is literally taking your power away from you! This will cause you stress.

Knowing what your story is takes courage and is the first step in creating new (and often dramatic) results. To be a passionate, goal-driven woman, it's vital to strip away the stories (excuses) so you can get to the heart of any fears or beliefs holding you back from your personal power zone.

~*Shifting the energy to work for you:* Is that possible? Start by identifying where your energy goes. Write down a typical day's activities or create a to-do list for uncompleted projects. Write down the feelings attached to the items that create the most stress and then identify the feelings you'd have if you were able to complete each of them. This allows you to change the way you think about the task or item. Then use the positive energy from accomplishing an item as a motivation versus the daunting feeling around the need to do it. Consider viewing the problems you face as an opportunity for you to develop more skills and to be a better person.

~Understand which phase you are in and how to work with it: Discovery phase – You are assessing options, ideas, plans, and are not yet committed but are striving to get clear so you can take action. Here you can set a "by when" date and make an assessment when you get there if you are ready to move into the action phase or if you should set a new date. Action phase – You are ready to take steps; you feel it, breathe it, your creative mind is on and you see possibilities, you are in motion and ready for more. Make sure you have a clear plan so you can measure and celebrate your progress as you implement. Be open to support and adjusting as needed. Stalled – You are unable to make decisions and feel resistance to try to do so. You are not motivated yet to make changes or take action.

Consider if it is the task or the overall goal you are not committed to that is causing this or if it involves belief in yourself. You can use the strategies in this book to help you move past the outer or inner blockers and get into the much more productive discovery state.

~Just breathe: This is often underrated but it helps oxygen get to your brain and releases tension in your body. Sit in a comfy chair, put relaxing music on, practice slow, deep breathing and focus on breathing in calm energy. Set a timer so you can really focus for five minutes and not short change yourself or be distracted. Just noticing if you are holding your breath helps to slow you down and calm you.

~Give yourself permission to acknowledge how you feel: Don't try to analyze it. Just notice it. Slow down and don't try to pretend it isn't so. Then write down what is stressing you out. You may be unaware of it until you write it down and see it for what it is. This will help you see a starting point to make a plan. Readjust today's agenda if needed so you can

achieve what is most important and shift your energy to feel good about it.

~Do something that makes you feel good: Shift your mental energy and the body will follow. Focus on something that helps you feel strong and able to take things on. Take a walk and breathe in the fresh air; let your mind wander. Put on a funny movie and laugh, read a favorite book or passages or call your coach for a quick "power up"! Positively stimulating one of your five senses will help shift your stress level and your reactions.

Work-Life Balance

Balance means different things to each of us. However, for most of us, one of the biggest barriers to achieving this sought after work-life balance is time. More specifically, a lack of time for the things that are important to us.

How to recognize if work-life balance is a problem for you:

When we feel "off balance" we feel like we are not in control, not doing the things we want to do or not moving at the pace we want. Take the example of a bicycle wheel. The spokes all meet evenly at the center, which creates the driving core energy and allows the wheel to move forward. The tire and rim hold all of the spokes together and allow the rider to balance on top and glide over terrain.

If our spokes (our priorities) are uneven, we will not have balance. If our core energy is not coming from our values, we will not move forward in the direction we want. How does your wheel feel? Is your ride bumpy, wobbly, smooth, or fast?

Ideas to create balance:

If you're like most women, career and professional development can take up a disproportionate amount of time and energy. Especially when you consider that it's only one of eight "life areas" that need your attention.

Take a moment to define what balance means to you in each of the life areas in the Wheel of Possibilities on the following page. Rate yourself on a scale of 1-10 (1=least satisfied, 10=most satisfied) of where you are TODAY in each of these areas. Do so by circling the number in each section. Now draw a line, starting in one section all the way around, connecting the numbers, and making your wheel.

What does your wheel look like? Could you balance on it, go very fast, or make it up steep hills?

The Wheel of Possibilities!

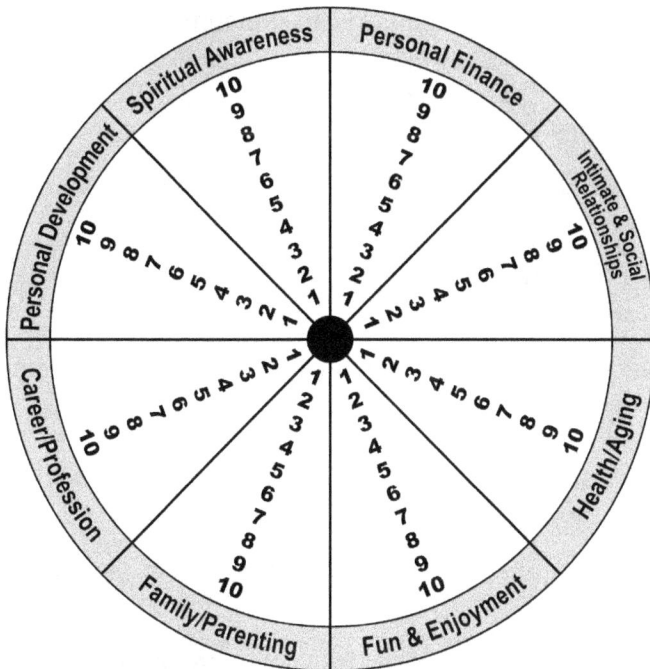

What possibilities do you see to create a balanced life?

As you work through the CRES System, you can integrate into your goals areas you want to enhance, and work to make your wheel even. Having all 5s is better than having a 10 in one area, and 2 and 3 in others. Even when you have a 10, your wheel can still be stretched out of shape if other areas have a much lower score. Work first on the areas that have the lowest score since changing these will make the biggest difference.

Rewards – Celebrating Success

Celebrating success is your right!

As professional women we can sometimes be so focused on the next result that we fail to make time to celebrate what we achieved. You can't afford not to as it <u>will</u> deplete your motivating energy.

How to recognize when you're NOT celebrating your success:

- You move onto another task before you celebrate your achievement.

- You don't allow others to acknowledge or validate you.

- You're the first to say, "It's no big deal."

- You don't take time to acknowledge or reward your team or support system.

- You might feel that your work or others' work is never enough.

- You might even think it is not appropriate to "toot your own horn" or give yourself credit.

Do any of these look familiar to you, or perhaps you have observed them in those you lead?

Remember—"Behind every successful woman is her most powerful self!" Are you behind yourself cheering yourself on?

Ideas to celebrate success:

~Reward yourself daily: Give yourself permission to celebrate when you reach a goal or each small step towards your goal. Simple rewards bring big paybacks. The following are suggestions for little ways to reward yourself: step outside and breath fresh air after working for two hours

on a project; listening to a favorite CD during your next work push; stop at a designated cutoff time; buy your favorite coffee, sipping it slowly; call a good friend, or better yet, meet her for lunch; or create a point system and with bigger projects work toward a larger reward like a weekend out of town or going to an upcoming concert.

~Invite others to celebrate with you: Use getting together as the reward. Practice acknowledging others and encourage them to celebrate too. Pay attention to how those around you respond to their success and even yours. Are you allowing or not?

~Recognize the good things that happened today: Start keeping track of the good things that happen in your day, right from the start; things you can celebrate that you took part in or achieved. Keep a running list and add to it each time something makes the list. In a bad moment, you can use this tool to reflect back on the good things that have happened. As insignificant as they may seem at the time, in a difficult moment they can help shift your perspective. Make it a game and see how many positive things you can find. Practice seeing the positive and what is working to help you reach your next level of success. Bonus Tip: When you get home at night and are asked how your day was, share your list instead of going into what didn't go right.

~Use your journal: Practice acknowledging yourself and celebrating your daily successes, no matter how small. This is a powerful habit for self-awareness and staying tapped into your power zone. This will also help you recognize what holds you back and what is affecting your drive and outcomes. Make a goal to do this for 30 days. Then plan a reward to celebrate your new habit. For extra credit, evaluate yourself. Do you see yourself focusing on the negative aspects or do you see yourself growing and shifting your perspective?

~*Take 5:* Connect with your personal power that allows you to get things done. Take five minutes a day to totally stop, breathe, relax, center, and appreciate yourself and your life. Practice letting go of other people's standards and expectations. If necessary, create a new score card for yourself to acknowledge and validate what you are doing right. We don't do enough of this!

(Refer to Step 10 in the FAP process for more reasons why celebrating success is so important.)

Self-Care Reservoir

In the pursuit of achieving your vision of success, it is especially important to take care of your health. Good health is more than just the absence of illness. Rather, it is the state of your physical and emotional well-being, acknowledging the importance and inseparability of our mind/body relationship. Building up your "self-care reservoir" can make you more productive, rather than self-destructive, when dealing with the pressures and demands you face.

How to recognize when your reservoir needs filled up:

- You constantly sacrifice your own needs to take care of everyone else.

- You put off your own self-care until "later" only "later" never comes.

- It seems like you are forever in a crisis or recovering from a crisis. You're never quite on solid ground.

- You feel like you are caught in a vicious cycle.

- You end up feeling resentful, unbalanced, stressed out, and unequipped to handle life's fast pace.

- This stress and lack of confidence influences everything from the quality of your relationships to your success in business.

Ideas for Filling up your Self-Care Reservoir

One of the bonuses for filling up your self-care reservoir is increasing your resilience. Resilience is a quality that is worth developing. When a woman is resilient, she's able to:

- Quickly recover from a set back

- Learn from every experience, both positive and negative

- Stay calm even when things feel out of control

- Accept when things don't go her way

Just imagine the confidence a woman with resilience feels. Would you like to feel some of that? Self-care is the answer. Do this by filling up your self-care reservoir.

A great way to begin filling your self-care reservoir is to look at what you can ADD to your life, specifically, activities or routines that you enjoy, find relaxing or increases your positive outlook. One such activity is exercise. By simply adding 15-30 minutes every 2 to 3 days you will experience several mental and physical benefits that will refill your reservoir.

Keep it simple and aim to add one new activity at a time. Schedule it into your calendar as often as you can – five minutes a day doing the right activity can do wonders for your sense of well-being. When you use the suggestions in time management strategy, you will create opportunities for this.

For bonus points, combine two pleasurable activities into one such as walking with a good friend, reading outside in the sunshine, or taking a bath while listening to your favorite music. Commit to keeping your self-care appointments. They're the most important entries in your calendar!

Another to consider is: Setting clear expectations with your children and family. As a professional woman and mother, you often find yourself being pulled in many directions. You might find that you give into unrealistic demands and set poor boundaries because of feelings of guilt and trying to balance your personal and professional lives. This causes a negative cycle of neglect that will create a domino effect. If you give away opportunities for self-care, you'll end up being no good to anyone, and it will take longer to refill your self-care reservoir. Setting limits and taking regular "me" time is important. Plus, you'll be setting a powerful example of self-worth and how to create balance.

Wrapping up:

Self-care is the oil of your life. It is not a luxury, it is a necessity! You will not be able to lead your life confidently from the power zone if you don't practice this strategy.

When you travel by plane, you are asked to look at the safety/ emergency instructions card. This gives specific instructions of what to do in the event of an emergency including what you should do if you're traveling with a child. It doesn't tell you to put the oxygen mask on your child first, but to put your mask on first. Why is that? So you don't pass out and then can't help your child. As professional women, we need to remember to put on our own oxygen masks before we give all the oxygen away to our children (others' demands, errands, projects, etc.). You are deserving of self-care. You will feel better, look better, rest better and, as a result, be less stressed and able to meet challenges head on and celebrate many more successes. If you have forgotten what it's like to feel refreshed and taken care of, start by getting in touch with your power zone. Close your eyes, take deep breaths, listen to your higher self and repeat, I am worthy. Once you feel her, commit to taking care of her and doing something about it.

The qualities you will develop as you commit to self-care:

Risk-taking—Self-assuredness—Assertiveness—Resilience

The challenges you will overcome from the CRES Score:

- Fatigue ("I feel tired all of the time")
- Mental fogginess ("I have trouble concentrating")
- Stress ("Some days I feel so stressed out!")
- Overwhelm ("Some days I feel down and wonder if all this work is worth it")
- Poor health ("I know that my health and well-being need more attention")

Now you're ready to deal with this final type of confidence blocker. Start by coming up with one self-care "action step" that would make a difference to your stress reaction, work/life balance, celebrating your success, or filling your self-care reservoir.

_____

You'll add this to the fourth row of your CRES Worksheet.

© The CRES Worksheet	Day:	Week:	Month:
Strategy One: Identify and Overcome Fears	My Action Step:	My Progress Notes:	
My CRES Score is:			Rating: 1 2 3 4 5 6 7 8 9 10
Possible 30			
Strategy Two: Remove Internal Barriers	My Action Step:	My Progress Notes:	
My CRES Score is:			Rating: 1 2 3 4 5 6 7 8 9 10
Possible 30			
Strategy Three: Unleash Your Assertiveness	My Action Step:	My Progress Notes:	
My CRES Score is:			Rating: 1 2 3 4 5 6 7 8 9 10
Possible 60			
Strategy Four: Commit to Self-Care	My Action Step:	My Progress Notes:	
My CRES Score is:			Rating: 1 2 3 4 5 6 7 8 9 10
Possible 50			

The CRES Worksheet Instructions

My CRES Score: At the beginning of the book, you assessed your current CRES score in each strategy and identified what you could benefit most from working on. Write the scores you got here. As you apply the steps, you can take the assessment again and see how you have improved and which strategy you could focus more on next time.

My Action Step: Next, write in each strategy the item you identified that was standing in the way of you taking risks to grow or blocking your confidence. Then, using the suggestions given in each strategy, or combining them with your own ideas, write out what you will do to overcome the confidence blocker. Make a commitment to carry out an action step that will support you in achieving your Vision of Success.

My Progress Notes: Evaluate how you did in applying the strategies. Did you get the results you wanted? What could you benefit from doing differently or more of? How could you improve your results? Did you feel more confident throughout your day? If you didn't, then what part of your action step can you fine-tune and try again? Don't be too quick to change your action step. Rather, see what prevented you from taking the step and work on resolving that in your plan. Re-commit to keep working on this action step until your target date or until you achieve your goal. This will build trust in you and, in turn, increase your confidence to take on the next necessary risk to grow.

Rating: Measure your progress each day by evaluating how satisfied you are with your efforts and the results of achieving action steps in each strategy. Rate yourself on a scale of 1-10 (1=Least, 10=Most) and then add up your points for a daily score. The total possible for each day is 40. Keep in mind that not all days are going to be "10" days. Your goal is to work towards consistency and overall increased confidence to achieve your vision of success.

Daily: To support creating new habits and behaviors, I recommend that for the first two weeks you use this worksheet daily. Each day evaluate how well you did using each CRES strategy.

Weekly/Ongoing: After 1 to 2 weeks, if you see new habits or behaviors are forming, you can move to an overall evaluation for the week. If you slide back, review more often. If you see consistency, move to a monthly evaluation. Each time you choose another item from your Vision of Success to create a goal with, examine your Confidence Blockers that may hold you back and use the process again.

Chapter/CRES Wrap Up:

The strategies we've discussed in this chapter – Identify and Overcome Fears, Remove Internal Barriers, Unleash Your Assertiveness and Commit to Self-Care – all work together to build your confidence.

As your confidence builds, you're able to take the necessary risks that lead to your next level of success, one step at a time.

But beware, the opposite is also true. When you're not applying these strategies, you're not taking any risks, and this inaction will fuel your fears, validate your negative internal beliefs, diminish your level of assertiveness and leave you feeling unworthy of self-care.

The CRES Worksheet is a simple and yet extremely powerful tool that can be a constant barometer of your confidence level. By using the worksheet, you'll have immediate feedback of how you're doing, and a structure for refining your focus and actions.

Notice, as well, how the four strategies become integrated into your life. For example, it's only by unleashing your assertiveness and having a courageous conversation with your family that you'll be able to block off and protect time for your own self-care activities.

Similarly, only by having the courage and awareness to examine your thought patterns and internal barriers can you recognize and deal with your fears as they come up. With this system, you can immediately see where you got off track, or where you stopped applying the CRES strategies.

The CRES System requires you to stretch yourself and leave your comfort zone, trust yourself, face the unknown, tune-in to your power, show up and claim what you want, living by choice instead of by reaction.

Chapter Five

Power Zone Principle #5

Understand the Qualities of a Confident Woman

"You've got to take the initiative and play your game. In a decisive set, confidence is the difference."

—*Chris Evert*

Tapping into the Qualities of a Confident Woman

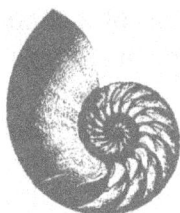

"You have to have confidence in your ability, and then be tough enough to follow through."

—Rosalynn Carter

As you work to apply the Power Zone Principles you have learned so far, you'll overcome the confidence blockers, go after your goals, take necessary risks to change, and see yourself moving closer to your vision of success. This will naturally increase your level of confidence and support you leaving your comfort zone. It also allows you to take advantage of developing several new qualities or fine-tuning ones you already possess.

When you're leading your life from the power zone, you are not afraid to demonstrate on the outside the confidence you feel on the inside. Because of this, you will show up differently. What I mean is, my clients at this phase share similar stories of being told that they look different, but those who comment on it aren't sure exactly why. My clients and I know it's because of the way they now carry themselves and honor themselves in their actions. They are living authentically and fully engaged in their lives, accessing their gifts and talents and the confidence found in their power zones.

Tapping into the qualities of a confident woman that await you in the power zone is an exciting and empowering experience. It can also pose some challenges if you are not familiar with how to use this newfound confidence. In this chapter, we will review the top 10 qualities of a confident woman and address why you may use them in some areas of your life and not in others and how they can work for or against you.

Take a moment to review the list of the Top 10 qualities identified below. Do you recognize yourself in any of these? Can you identify with areas where you are not quite there yet but wish you were? Do you ever find yourself sometimes using these and sometimes not?

Top Ten Qualities of a Confident Woman

She's a **RISK-TAKER.**

She steps past her fear and reaches for the success that's waiting for her beyond it.

She's **RESILIENT.**

She bounces back and learns from things that didn't go as planned.

She's **PERSISTENT.**

She stays on her path to success despite any obstacles, doubts, or challenges.

She's **SELF-ASSURED.**

She acknowledges and expresses pride in what she's good at.

She's **CREATIVE.**

She can see alternate perspectives and think "outside of the box."

She's **RESOURCEFUL.**

She seeks out support and information when she needs them.

She's **SELF-RELIANT.**

She has a strong sense of self-worth that's based on internal measures.

She's **ASSERTIVE.**

She has clear boundaries and teaches people how to respect them.

She's **INTUITIVE.**

She has faith in her own judgment and is deeply tuned in to her higher self.

She's **FLEXIBLE.**

She's open to new ideas and capable of adapting to change.

(Note: These are the qualites you will develop using the CRES System.)

The mask of confidence

As a successful professional woman, you obviously have many positive qualities. Sometimes that makes it all the more perplexing when you get stuck. Because if you have all of these wonderful qualities, why haven't you been able to fulfill your vision of success?

The first reason is that you've been unable to apply the qualities across all areas of your life. For instance, I heard someone at a women's business networking event say that, while she's very assertive about speaking her mind at work, it's difficult to do so in her relationships. Another woman shared that she employs military precision to organize her household but her desk at work is a black hole of lost files. And I often hear women say how at work, they are able to take risks and inspire others and meet their goals, but in their personal life, they hold themselves back, are fearful of taking risks, are often disorganized, and don't feel inspired or motivated.

Why is it that we use our confidence in some areas and not in others? We're bound to feel more confident in some areas. And we've had more chances to practice skills in certain areas. The skills and talents that allow us to act with confidence don't leave us; rather, we are choosing, sometimes unconsciously, to use them or not.

The less confident we feel, the more likely we are to put on a "mask" of confidence instead and the less likely we are to stretch out of our comfort zone (potentially making a mistake or looking foolish) by trying something new or practicing a skill, so we stay put.

This isn't the "fake it until you make it" scenario where you dig in and do your best, determined to grow and make something work. Because in those cases at least you're taking a risk to do something different.

However, the downside of this scenario is that you are keeping all the anxieties to yourself. Your energy is going inward to stay looking composed as you painstakingly figure out what to do and the side effect of this is you could potentially miss out on allowing someone to mentor you, which could speed up your growth process and open doors to more opportunity.

Confident women don't have all the answers and they too lack confidence!

Why do we wear the mask?

Have you ever admired another woman's confidence as you watched her making a speech, performing on stage or television, shaking hands on a huge deal or handling a challenging situation with grace and kindness?

Our perception is that she has it all together and she knows it. However, it's important to realize that no matter how much confidence we exude outwardly, we ALL sometimes doubt our decisions and capabilities.

Certainly self-reliance is an essential quality of a confident woman. However, the woman who uses her confidence to achieve business success is one who has a balance of qualities. The quality of self-reliance needs to be balanced with the quality of resourcefulness or the willingness and wisdom to ask for help.

Certain situations can block our confidence, making us less willing to risk stepping out of our comfort zone. Some of these situations could be easily managed if we were to draw on outside sources of information and support.

For instance, your manager has asked you to write a report about an area of the company you're not very familiar with. You may choose to be self-reliant and try to figure it out for yourself. You might be concerned with other people's perceptions of you and you definitely don't want to admit that you don't know everything.

In doing so, you're choosing to wear a mask of confidence, while inside you're doubting yourself and worrying about being "found out." That's a recipe for high stress that can quickly become overwhelming!

Or, you could make an appointment to meet with someone in that department and learn more about what goes on there.

And it's seeking out help, information, resources, and support that's going to move you forward.

Being a confident woman doesn't mean you have all the answers. It means you're secure enough to seek out the people, resources, and solutions you need to overcome obstacles and challenges.

It means that you invite others' support, listen thoughtfully and with an open mind, and then determine whether or not that advice will help you to fulfill your vision of success.

It also means you are not threatened by other confident women who could lend you advice or mentor you, and as a result, you benefit from opportunities to collaborate.

I have spoken on this principle, the "mask of confidence", several times. One event in particular that stands out in my mind was in 2006 at the University of Utah's David Eccles School of Business, where I spoke to a group of over 150 professionals. When the host introduced me and my "odd topic" with a note of humor, I could feel the curiosity awaken in the room. For the next hour, as the presentation unfolded, I sensed the energy this "odd topic" created, and watched the "aha" moments happen as the audience identified with the mask they didn't even realize they had. This was inspiring to me as well.

What I call the "mask of confidence" is perhaps something you've experienced in your life with your career, peers, employees, relationships or in your family. When you uncover why you use your confidence in some areas and not in others, and identify what your mask is made of, you'll be able to unleash the power you possess when it's removed.

What is the mask?

It's a self-imposed protective barrier blocking your personal power. It's a way we suppress ourselves and limit our gifts, talents, and strengths. It lessens our ability to honor ourselves because it diminishes our willingness to see our weaknesses as opportunities to grow, rather than something to hide from. It can be fueled by denial most often caused by fears of success or failure. This prevents us from taking responsibility to step past our current comfort zone and stop acting as if all is okay although it is not. We also tell ourselves we're okay with the way we are treated, or with an outcome of a situation, though we know it's against our values.

We addressed the importance of your values in the vision of success chapter and how when your decisions go against your fundamental values, it creates internal conflict and affects your desire and willingness to take action. When you are wearing the mask, you'll find yourself tolerating and justifying, and you'll end up feeling guilty because you are not honoring your values. This lessens your ability to take off the mask and give yourself permission to grow. You are treading water at this point and hoping your mask doesn't fall off and expose the panic underneath.

What is the mask made of?

Confidence Blockers. These confidence blockers are very powerful, and as we reviewed in the earlier chapter, they limit our ability to trust ourselves and take necessary risks to grow – in essence, allow ourselves to show up as who we are, no matter what others think, what we perceive they may think, or how we assume they may judge us.

The mask limits our power to authentically express ourselves. I have seen it prevent others we influence from reaching toward their greatness because we are leading by a false example. We cannot be fully in touch with our power zone when we are wearing our mask, because it prevents us from using our personal greatness and core driving energy, fueled by our values.

Sometimes we'll peek from behind the mask, testing the waters and take it on and off in different situations, usually without even recognizing we are doing this. We might have a limiting belief that if we took it off, we would let everyone down, or we'd have to face how we really feel about ourselves.

When I work with new clients in my supporting Power Zone Mastery™ Program, I generally find that this mask is present in some form. Even though they may not be aware of their own mask, they are aware of their feelings of conflict. They may not trust their personal power or are afraid others won't accept them if they show their stronger, more confident selves.

Client example: How she has noticed the mask in her life.

When she's not wearing the mask, she recognizes and takes ownership of her responsibility, feels her power to show up 100 percent, feels in control, makes choices that align with her values, and gives herself permission to grow. When she is wearing the mask, she ignores her responsibility to show up; things run her, and she doesn't make proactive choices. In addition, when wearing the mask, she admits to avoiding areas of weakness, looking only at strengths, but that causes weaknesses to gain more energy and power because in avoiding them, they get larger than they really are. And this diminishes her strengths and depletes her overall motivating energy to take off the mask.

Confidence blockers are dictating behaviors and choices, which diminish her personal power; the opposite is true when she takes it off and shows up in all her glory — her confidence and her personal power to choose increase.

What are the effects of the mask?

When wearing it, you're less likely to stretch out of your comfort zone, can be indifferent to growth, and are less likely to try something new or practice a skill. Sneaky self-sabotaging is taking place, which reinforces beliefs and habits that are not necessarily healthy. It prevents asking for help or receiving support, which can reinforce the myth that confident women must have all the answers and do it all on their own.

It affects our ability to trust ourselves and to make choices that align with our values. Not wearing the mask requires you

to stretch yourself and leave your comfort zone, believe in your higher self, take a risk to expose yourself first and foremost to you, face the unknown, tune in to your power, show up, and claim what you want. Removing the mask is essential to living an empowered, fulfilling, and purposeful life.

What is the power that unleashes when the mask is removed?

Removing the mask provides direct access to your power zone which increases belief in yourself and in your ability to achieve your true goals and live your full potential. As a result, you are open to developing new qualities and skills.

You'll be able to rely on your skills at all times. You'll no longer have to "change hats" when you enter an unfamiliar situation or when you switch between your personal and professional lives. Your best skills will be integrated so deeply into your personality that they will shine through whenever and wherever you need them.

You'll be able to notice whether those around you are wearing the mask of confidence, (avoiding, denial, acting as if everything's okay though they're in conflict) and while working to use your confidence in all areas, you'll lead by example. It's easier for you to take the necessary risks to do things differently, which will give you the results you truly desire and deserve.

Key point: When we can clearly present who we are, we can ultimately attain our greatest goals!

What's working for or against you?

The second reason that having these positive qualities isn't enough is that one or more of these qualities may have a downside that is working against you.

When you understand the qualities of a confident woman, you can begin pinpointing exactly what is working for you and what is working against you in order to fine tune and individualize the strategies to work in YOUR life.

Here are three of the qualities and an example of each working for or against a confident woman:

She's a Risk-Taker. She isn't afraid to recognize and take bold steps past her fear because she knows that success lies just over the horizon.

She's Resilient. When things don't go according to plan, she is able to bounce back and learn from it, instead of running from it.

She's Persistent. She doesn't let obstacles push her off her success path.

When these qualities are working for you, you build powerful momentum toward your goals. But when they are working against you, it can set some dangerous precedents into motion.

For instance, if you have *Risk-Taking* working against you, you may lose interest as your ideas or plans begin to work, which can compromise your ability to follow through, resulting in a step backward instead of forward.

If *Resilience* is working against you, you may not allow yourself enough time for self-care.

If *Persistence* is working against you, you may be unwilling to shift, become indignant, and are unable to make the adjustments necessary to succeed at a faster pace.

Can you see how the same quality can have a positive or an adverse affect?

Before I discuss this concept further, take time now to consider if any of these qualities are working against YOU:

Quality	How it may be working against you
Risk Taker	May lose interest as things start working, feel less excitement and have difficulty with follow through
Resilient	May not allow for enough self-care
Persistent	May be stubborn and not shift
Self-assured	May be over-confident or have blind spots
Creative	May feel overwhelmed, overloaded with ideas, too stuck to begin
Resourceful	May not collaborate, overly dependent on self

Self-reliant	May isolate and not seek out or accept support
Assertive	May come across too strongly and be difficult to approach
Intuitive	May leap in without enough planning or consideration of potential challenges
Flexible	May steer away from planned schedule

What is the effect when the qualities work against you?

When any of the qualities are working against you, they can make it harder on you, such as not being perceived the way you would like to be perceived and not getting the response you want. Additionally, you might not be allowing support, becoming discouraged and ending up not following through. You might be trying too hard because you are not comfortable with your skills and are not quite sure how to create a pleasant balance with the qualities.

Years ago, I had to address the way I was communicating, as I wasn't being received the way I intended. As a result, I would sometimes offend or rub people the wrong way when I thought I was just being assertive or self-assured. My heart was full of good intentions, and I really didn't mean to come across this way. At first, it wasn't easy to take a hard look at how I was using a few qualities against myself. I admit I felt a little defensive at first. However, with my coach's help, I could turn things around and get my message across, creating the positive reaction of collaboration and enthusiasm for my ideas I wanted to share.

I have also seen how devastating it can be to a company, employees, and personal support systems, like family and friends, when a woman in a role of leadership doesn't see or want to admit her blind spot, when one or more of the qualities are working against her. She has to work extra hard on the inside overcoming her insecurities because she can't allow anyone to see she has doubts, or isn't as strong as she presents herself. As she puts on her mask, she has to act like she has it all together, but it's usually pretty transparent to others and has the reverse effect of exuding confidence and inspiring others to rally around and support her. In worst cases, she can unknowingly prevent others around her from growing past her own comfort level and is generally seen as controlling, demanding, and not trustworthy.

What if you could shift your perception and get a different result?

In the story above, because she is living in the myth that confident women have all the answers and don't need support, she gives off this message to others, preventing her from being a role model for change and personal growth. So much negative, mental draining energy goes into trying to portray this image. Most likely, to be in a role of leadership she has the skills and talents to be there but has forgotten how to use the qualities of the confidence that got her there to truly shine as an empowered leader. Limiting beliefs are suppressing her true greatness as she keeps reinforcing the myth.

What if she could see that asking for help is a strength, that asking is a form of giving, the gift of allowing someone to serve and to use their own personal power zone? She would eliminate isolation, feeling stressed out, making herself responsible for everything without much-needed support. If she could eliminate the need to be right, face her fears, and the limiting belief that others might think she is stupid if she can't figure it out on her own just imagine the power she could access.

How can the qualities be misinterpreted?

Another situation to consider is when a woman misinterprets how to use her confidence or a particular quality in either her personal or professional life.

If you are not getting the reactions you want, perhaps you feel like you might have to explain yourself and are constantly working harder than you think you should, then be open to ask a close friend, mentor, or your coach to help you assess how you are showing up with your qualities.

Which ones are working for or against you? Where could you adjust and create a harmonious balance instead of resistance? What would happen if you gave yourself permission to grow without fear of what others would think?

This could allow you to be on the inside what others perceive on the outside or create greater results and have higher levels of confidence to access.

Wrapping up:

Use your own personal barometer – simply put, it is a reflection of how you feel on the inside and how those around you react to you on the outside. The slightest adjustments can make the greatest difference and increase your energy rather than drain it. Let go of your need to be right and pay attention to any resistance you are getting. Embrace areas you need to work on so that you can release any negative hold they have on you and create a solid foundation to leverage your qualities.

How energized, confident, and driven do you think you'll be when things start to click for you in this area? How motivated to succeed will you be when you've identified what can be worked on and what can be set free?

If you find it hard to get one or more of the qualities to work for you and are not getting the results you desire, refer to the four confidence blockers and determine which one is holding you back, and then use the CRES worksheet to move past it.

As you apply the principles in this book, get comfortable with regular self-assessment and increasing your risk tolerance to change. Resist the tolerance factor to make excuses that you'll do this someday. Take off your blinders and remove your mask, then adjust your qualities to work for you, and finally, enjoy your newfound confidence on your journey to success!

Chapter Six

Power Zone
Principle #6

Become an Empowered Leader

"Before you are a leader, success is all about growing yourself.
When you become a leader, success is all about growing others."
— Jack Welch

Your Personal Leadership Journey

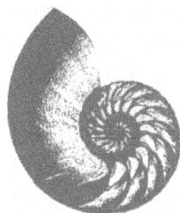

"There is no passion to be found playing small - in settling for a life that is less than the one you are capable of living."

—*Nelson Mandela*

As you apply the Power Zone Principles, you will gain confidence and increase belief in your capabilities and capacity to grow. This causes your personal greatness to further awaken, intensifying the internal desire and calling you to become a leader in all areas of your life. This will be an amazing transformation for you! The possibilities of the power zone lay before you and it's no longer sufficient to use the gifts you have discovered just for yourself.

In this chapter, I will address your next growing opportunity, your personal leadership journey and how to take it to the next level in your professional life. We spend so much of our time at work that it only makes sense, in keeping with the goal to be authentic and show up 100 percent, that you understand how to use your new confidence and skills in the other half of your life.

As a professional woman, whether in a role of leadership (business owner, executive, manager, or team lead) or as an emerging leader (learning to lead yourself or support your co-workers), one of the greatest gifts you'll receive from leaving your comfort zone will be to inspire others to their greatness through your own ability to lead your life in the direction of your journey to success.

This means your success hinges on your leadership abilities in ALL areas of your life, starting with taking charge of your journey to success and showing up powerfully.

A woman who shows up powerfully is someone who has learned to tap into her power zone, uses it to consciously fulfill her purpose, and is willing to take on leadership roles using her newfound courage and confidence to thoughtfully impact others. It doesn't matter if it is in her profession or business, or in a service capacity, so long as she is in tune with and aware of her gifts so she can use them for the greater good.

Becoming an empowered leader in all areas of your life will afford you many worthwhile rewards, such as not having to wear the mask of confidence we focused on previously, and opening up possibilities to serve and be deeply enriched beyond your imagination.

Becoming an empowered leader is not always an easy thing to do. As with any new skill or habit, sometimes we can get off course, lose sight, and forget to use our personal greatness. You might be in a situation where you acquired the role by default. For example, perhaps you receive notice for successfully completing a large project and are asked to lead the next one, but not because you aspired to lead others. Or you may not realize how others naturally see you as a role model, watching your actions and listening to your words, seeking to be like you. It is important to recognize if you are acting out of a default leadership style versus by intention so you can shift this "default" status into powerful intentions for good.

Becoming an empowered leader means you must connect with the "honorable" part of leadership; in essence, you must honor the influence you have. When you're in any capacity to influence others, you'll have more opportunities to draw on your strengths, talents and use the principles you are learning. In this role, there should be a raised consciousness and accountability about the positive impact you can have.

Since we all have the ability to set an example, good or bad, being true to our power within is an essential ingredient to lead, empower, and influence others to their greatness. Don't take this for granted because not everyone can do it. Not everyone will be willing to take the necessary steps to leave their comfort zones and their limiting beliefs and behaviors to embrace transforming into the leader inside them.

Your ability to align your leadership with your "power zone" is to be cherished and shared. Your greatest gift in this role will be your ability to inspire others and then lead the change that you inspire.

One of my passions is to inspire each woman to step up into roles of leadership and honor her natural power to influence, so that all who follow her can see their own greatness in her eyes and take the leap of faith to become empowered leaders too.

By doing so, we can create a positive cycle that produces opportunities for all of us to experience a higher level of happiness and success.

With all you have learned thus far, you are poised to further stretch the boundaries of your comfort zone and take advantage of the opportunity to make a difference through leading by example. Do this for yourself first and foremost so that living the principles becomes naturally reflected in your actions and words. Each day remind yourself of the precious gift you received to become reacquainted with your power zone, or your higher self, and what it is allowing you to do and, most importantly, become. Stay in touch with your best self and act upon it.

In the next sections, we will dig into the three key elements necessary to become an Empowered Leader:

Finding Your Voice

Inspiring Change

Leading Change

My desire in exploring these elements is to help women like you to emerge as passionately empowered leaders in their life and work. As you go through the next sections, keep these questions in mind.

How do you define leadership, in life and in your work?

What kind of leader do you want to be?

What do you want to achieve through your leadership?

What drives your desire to lead?

Finding Your Voice

> *"A bird doesn't sing because it has an answer, it sings because it has a song."* —*Maya Angelou, writer*

When women are driven by their internal voice that encourages their desire to make a difference, they can inspire incredible changes for themselves and for others they influence. To do this, they must first trust themselves to recognize their own voice, their personal calling to serve, and boldly claim their passion and what makes them special.

Next they will need to value the gifts that come from claiming their voice and be willing to share and grow from using them. If they don't do this, they can lose touch with it, forget they have it, or, worse, keep seeking after it, not believing that they have found it.

Like it or not, women spend a great deal of time and energy on the pursuit of discovering their voice, wondering if they really found it or how to use it.

We are naturally drawn to find and fulfill our purpose. We are amazing creatures, and when we put our minds to it, we can do just about anything. However, we are also equally great at self-doubt and limiting beliefs, spending way too much time in self-defeating behaviors, like justifying our right to use our voice. We may even rationalize that we can't possibly be that great and talk ourselves right out of it, letting the voice go silent.

The seashell story

To illustrate this further, I would like to share an analogy with you. Imagine standing on a cliff looking out at a long, beautiful, silky beach with waves rolling up. You see tiny bursts of shimmering light with each wave splashing the sand that beckon you to come explore. There is only one way to get there though, through a steep, winding path, with thorny bushes and slippery rocks that line the pathway. Yet, even with these challenges you feel the quest calling you and you choose to set forth.

It's a tough descent — you even slip a few times and have to reach out and prop yourself back up from a near fall. You continue to forge ahead, getting more and more excited as the beach and the brilliance of the shimmering light grow closer.

As you descend to the bottom of the trail, you step out on the beach and make your way to where the waves touch the sand. To your amazement, you find that what you saw shimmering is a seashell being brought in by the waves. It's not just any seashell, but one so incredibly beautiful that you have never seen one like it before. However, the waves bring it in and just as quickly as it sparkles from catching a ray of sunshine so your eyes can focus on it, it is back out to sea. You must plan carefully and time it just right in order to grab it. You are smart, so you calculate your attack, and you are finally able to scoop up the remarkable seashell.

You take time to admire this beautiful treasure and can't wait to share it. You even feel a sense of liveliness and excitement as you hold it. You put it to your ear and swear you hear something calling you. You are in awe. Deep inside, you feel a strong sense of purpose welling up; you wonder if this is a special seashell, if perhaps it possesses a magical power that would allow you to do great things. Your thoughts shift as you notice the sun starting to set. You can't wait to share your rare find, so you put it in your pocket and start to make the hard climb back up the trail to head home.

With each step it's getting later and you start to think about all you have to do to before the day ends and you even ponder what tomorrow may bring. Your mind wanders away from your rare find, so it becomes a fleeting memory, just as quickly as you make your way home.

The opportunity to take advantage of this experience lies before you. The choice of what to do with this rare seashell and how it made you feel is also there.

What will you do?

Do you find this beautiful seashell and put it in your pocket only to rush home with thoughts of your busy life? Do you start to think, "This is foolish. I've wasted so much time when there have to be so many other beautiful seashells out there. Mine is not really all that special; I should just forget about it?"

Or perhaps you take it home and hurriedly empty your pocket to set it on a shelf, but forget to share it over the next few weeks or months when people come to visit. Before you share it, perhaps you might even be planning to go out again and keep looking for another seashell just a little more perfect than this one, not realizing that what you already possess is so rare there is not another one like it.

Or do you recognize its value and choose to share it with others? In doing so, you tell the story about finding it, overcoming the adversity to get to the beach and climb the trail back home. You show the seashell and tell how it made you feel when you held it in your hands and to your ear. You share the energy and inspiration the seashell brought, and while doing so, something magical happens as it shines into your listeners' faces, illuminating and exciting their desire to find their own seashell. This inspires you to help them plot out their course to do so.

What's the moral of the story?

The seashell represents stepping out of your protective shell (the comfort zone) and claiming your voice. It sometimes shows itself in surprising and unexpected ways. When you find yours, it feels magical and exciting all at the same time. It feels like something mysterious and special is inside of you. The energy and connection you find will drive you into action, inspiring you to want to make a difference and increase the volume of your voice. It can create connections with people you never thought possible. It can cultivate your talents and ignite passion and purpose. It pushes you past your boundaries, with little to no resistance because it feels easy and natural. You'll feel it deep inside; it's like an awakening of your dormant true self.

Questions to ask yourself to awaken your voice:

What do you believe in?

What do you stand for?

What are you passionate about?

What drives your desire to inspire change?

What are you willing to go to the edge for?

What is your voice telling you?

The journey you embark upon after discovering your seashell demonstrates whether you're allowing your light to shine in spite of everyday challenges or in the face of real adversity, and whether you've conquered the limiting belief that "there are many seashells rarer than mine, so why should mine matter?"

Will you be driven by your voice? Will you make a difference? Will you overcome fears of failure or success? Will you trust in your voice?

Getting in touch with your powerful internal voice comes from practicing self-awareness and by recognizing and tapping into your power zone, where your unique gifts await you. Understanding how to find your voice allows you to stay in tune with your personal passion and driving core energy anytime you want. You can propel yourself into powerful action, literally transforming your life and the lives of those around you by finding and staying in tune with your unique voice.

The charge I leave you with is:

You must not be afraid to let your voice guide your life. Share the story of your journey, including adversity you've overcome, to help others find theirs.

You must not fall into the trap of thinking that you are not all that special or that everyone else understands what makes them special too. Just think — if it's hard for you to grasp this concept or stay tapped into your voice, imagine what it is like for those you lead who have less confidence or belief in their abilities and gifts.

In order to be a leader, you must be willing to take risks, challenge your comfort zone, and share your voice. This will support your efforts to practice showing up 100 percent and allow you to be less self-conscious or even less defensive about your uniqueness and passion to lead. Especially if you are an emerging leader, this step is essential.

As an empowered leader, it's your responsibility to exercise your voice and identify your personal value in areas such as service and leadership roles in the workplace. You cannot drive your personal vision forward and fulfill your purpose without finding and sharing your own voice and value.

When you find your voice and share it with others, you will truly begin to become an inspiring influence. The power it unleashes is magical and is what drives me to share my voice with you!

Inspiring Change

"If your actions inspire others to dream more, learn more, do more and become more, you are a leader."
— *John Quincy Adams*

Inspiring others begins with using your inner voice to first inspire greater changes for yourself. Being a leader in your life allows you to expand your vision, assess the changes you want, and create bolder goals so you can confidently eliminate any blockers in your way. With calmness, grace and ease, you benefit from the qualities of a confident woman, forging a new future for yourself.

The energy and enthusiasm from inspiration will show in your countenance and the way you interact with others. Those around you will want what you have. Your happiness, peace, confidence, and energy for life will be infectious.

Use this gift, this power, to motivate and inspire others to find their voice and teach them how to apply the principles in their life. By doing so you can become a positive change factor for your organization or in areas where you serve.

In this section, we'll cover three things to help you inspire others:

- Power of influence (which woman are you?)
- Using delegation to inspire changes
- Role model self-disclosure

When you are in a position of influence such as a team manager, a leader of a department or an organization, you must use the strengths you have been given to inspire others to see their greatness in order to grow and contribute. In fact, it's your responsibility to help those you lead discover their untapped gifts and talents so they can overcome obstacles and support the larger vision you are trying to achieve. Through honoring the power of influence in your leadership and inspiring changes, you can create powerful shifts in your environment and in others.

By power of influence, I mean the ability to recognize the power within you that can be used to empower and positively challenge others to stretch beyond their comfort zones. This power can help them see their light, like in the analogy of the reflection from the seashell, which inspires them to create personal growth transformations. This can become one of the most personally fulfilling experiences you will ever be part of.

Unfortunately, in many cases, women can't see the leadership potential within themselves. It gets forgotten or they shrink from the responsibility when they could use it to accomplish so much good. When you understand who you are and the power and talents you have to help those around you, then the leader in you will awaken, and you'll start to create personal transformations too.

With the opportunity to lead comes the honor of the power of influence. I also sometimes refer to this as the "sign" you are truly becoming an Empowered Leader. The power of influence doesn't come by force but by tapping into your personal internal power and voice, and then leading and inspiring changes from the inside out. The "sign" will be in the way individuals react to you, the way they want to step up and serve, to emerge from their protective barriers or shells, to exemplify your actions and strive to be like you.

When you are honoring your gift of leadership you are seizing opportunities to serve others by helping them grow to their greatness by teaching and guiding them on how to evolve into what makes them special. In essence, you become the head cheerleader, championing them, showing the way to overcome obstacles and inspiring them to reach for their next level of success.

Which woman are you?

Each of the following examples presents a challenge and can say a lot about your understanding of the power of influence you have in your own life and the lives of those you lead.

The first woman would be the person who recognizes her influence and uses it to help others. She is someone people flock to because she empowers and uplifts those around her and refuses to let challenges stop her progression. In fact, she recognizes her challenges as defining moments that will only make her stronger, and she shares these experiences to encourage others with her personal journey. She is not afraid to show up and share her voice and value!

The second woman may identify the potential she has to lead and help others but is either unsure how to use it or has chosen not to. She may just need a little guidance. I would guess many of us fall into this category and that's okay. You know it's there and have felt it; perhaps you have even experienced serendipitous moments when you've aligned with it and felt driven to visions bigger than yourself. You just need courage and support to take intelligent risks to claim it and begin using it. Get excited because your transformation is about to happen. Imagine the possibilities!

The third woman has more of a challenge. She is the type who doesn't know who she is, perhaps is in her role by default, and doesn't recognize the power of influence within herself. It could be any number of factors that keep a woman from recognizing her gift to inspire including an inability to set proper boundaries, focusing her energy in the wrong areas, or not knowing how to tap into the power she has. If you find yourself in this group, don't despair! You can overcome your concerns and become the woman who confidently leads and inspires others. You just need to identify what is holding you back and keeping you from your greatness. Evaluating the confidence blockers will help you identify where to start. What are you waiting for?

Using delegation to inspire changes

I have found that many professional women face hindrances to their confidently leading and inspiring others. One of the most under appreciated and largely overlooked is the ability to successfully delegate. The skill to delegate is a necessity in any leadership role so that you can use your time more wisely to achieve the larger goals, including having the time to mentor and influence others to grow.

Two main reasons you may not be able to successfully delegate.

1) Lack of evaluating your responsibilities: Most women who are in busy roles don't take time to regularly assess and evaluate their responsibilities. Because of this, they can't see if the current tasks they are doing align with their leadership vision or professional goals. Determine whether the tasks necessary to achieve your objectives really require only your unique skills and abilities. If you find yourself feeling stalled, evaluate if you could be in a holding pattern.

What I refer to as a holding pattern is when you tell yourself that someday you'll get there, when this settles down or when that project is done. Then, you'll get organized, or you'll make it happen later when you have time. The many women who have these thoughts are holding back their ability to be productive and efficient with their responsibilities. In addition, it's holding back those they lead because if they were to do an evaluation and share their needs, they would find opportunities where they could inspire others to grow. Even if you start with delegating one part of a project, you will end up having more time and energy. You will inspire someone else to grow and as they continue to take on more, you'll build trust and reap the rewards of putting your focus on the right things and increasing your momentum.

2) Limiting beliefs about delegation: Another hindrance woman are typically challenged with is having a limiting belief that no one can do the task as well as they can. If this is you, I challenge you to evaluate your beliefs on delegation. Be realistic on what you really have control over. Get over the fear of having to be the only one to make decisions. It's easier to do so when you are in tune with yourself, as you'll process things differently and lead and guide from that position. Tell yourself that you don't have to always be in control. You can be more confident by allowing others to help serve your vision and by releasing those fears. When you use the delegation skill, you'll be able to set limits and evaluate where you want to put your focus and energy. You'll be able to clearly communicate your needs so you can stay informed, set guidelines for decision making, and, thus, remain proactive without needing to be in control of every step.

If you fall into the trap of limiting beliefs or find yourself in a holding pattern, challenge yourself to practice the strategies in the Unleashing Your Assertiveness section to help you shift. You can also refer to additional resources and programs I have available to support female leaders and small business owners.

Don't underestimate the importance of effective delegation. It's one of the leadership skills necessary to inspire others into action and ignite personal growth. You must be able to increase your assertiveness to speak up and to champion others in the process. If this is done in an honorable way, you can be proud that you are becoming an empowered leader. If you are on the receiving end of delegation, be open to step up, ask for, and be ready to receive the opportunity to grow.

Role model self-disclosure

"If you have knowledge, let others light their candles in it."
— *Margaret Fuller*

One of the myths I see preventing women in leadership roles from role model self-disclosure is the fear that their team members will lose confidence and respect in them. Nothing is further from the truth!

A team that is supported and lead by example to personally develop will view the leader with respect and credibility.

Where do you begin?

Share how you have grown in the past through your personal experiences such as defining moments and learning opportunities.

Share your willingness to continue to evaluate yourself and be open to constructive feedback.

Share how you have inspired yourself and continued to grow and develop in the face of difficulty or how you attribute your failures or lack of successes as learning opportunities.

You will set a powerful example and give others the permission to boldly face change!

Out of new trust and respect they'll have for you, they will be inspired to take risks and grow, they'll be less fearful to share their weaknesses with you, and you will discover what they need to succeed without all the guesswork.

A natural consequence of the new respect is improved behavior and open dialogue that allow for productive feedback. Not surprisingly, this will generally result in higher levels of performance, energy, and productivity and will accelerate your leadership objectives.

Some tips to help you practice this:

- Practice leading others by example.

- Promote an emotionally safe environment for feedback by sharing your desire to grow and learn.

- Share your appropriate experiences of growth and invite others to do the same.

- Be less protective, more open and honest, and demonstrate willingness to change.

Bonus: As a result, you will get to stay in touch with your power zone every day and not live in conflict.

Questions to ask yourself include:

- Are you allowing yourself to show up 100 percent as an empowered leader? Why or why not?

- How have you inspired others lately? How have you shared defining moments or challenged others to grow?

- What have you done to get to know yourself, your skills, your abilities, or innate strengths to effectively delegate?

- When you master inspiring change in yourself and then in others, you'll create opportunities to lead the change you want to see. You'll transform into an empowered leader. Honoring the power of influence is a key principle of leadership. Remember this requires self-awareness as you can't lead others if you don't know yourself. Once you learn to honor your power of influence, you'll increase your ability to notice others' greatness and help draw it out.

Leading Change

"A leader takes people where they want to go. A great leader takes people where they don't necessarily want to go, but ought to be." —Rosalynn Carter

This third element of empowered leadership, leading change, is where you combine your voice and the power of inspiration and influence to lead extraordinary changes in your life. Here everything comes full circle and you don't have one foot in and one foot out. Here you can make the biggest impact because you know how to access your higher self by working in the power zone.

This is an amazing time for you. In your personal life, you have witnessed your own transformation taking place. You are attracting opportunities, and creative ideas are flowing. You're attracting and exchanging energy with other like-minded, wonderful women. You are showing up, playing bigger and wanting to enlarge the vision in others. There is a positive force building inside you, in desperate need of an outlet. This force is the desire to serve though leadership and share your knowledge of what personal growth can do.

Here are three areas to consider when leading change:

- Leading the vision of others
- Walking your leadership talk (Role modeling personal growth)
- Why women make great leaders

Leading the vision of others

> *"The very essence of leadership is that you have a vision.*
> *You can't blow an uncertain trumpet."*
> —*Theodore M. Hesburgh*

Women in leadership have unique and personally-enriching roles, filled with many opportunities and successes. Yet, this role also presents challenging situations, and personal defining moments, requiring necessary risks, which at times result in less than desirable outcomes. It can be a double-edge sword, so to speak, with triumphs and challenges, gains and losses.

A leader carries much on her shoulders, not only being in charge of heavy responsibilities but also having to get the dayto-day agenda, projects, reports, and meetings done so that the business goals and objectives move forward. Leaders wear many hats and need to be innovative and build relationships of trust to help those they lead embrace the changes.

Being a successful leader will require enlisting the help of others and one powerful way is through "leading the vision" of others. Leading the vision of others means that your team, employees, or support system, have to see themselves as part of the larger vision. This will get them excited to work the vision which is necessary or you will spend much of your time telling, convincing, and even demanding versus leading, inspiring, guiding, and celebrating success.

Leading the vision of others is not an easy task. Given the very nature of the role, it's easy to become too focused on just getting the job done, which often neglects opportunities to mentor and inspire others to achieve their personal greatness. This is a key point to recognize because when we don't make time to mentor others, we miss opportunities to lighten our load as we benefit from their talents and strengths. We also miss benefits that come from collaboration and increased support and resources to carry out the larger responsibilities. We'll most likely end up feeling like we are pulling or pushing others because they don't understand the greater vision and their part in it.

If you fall into this category, you may be feeling drained and isolated which lessens your motivation and confidence. It can also make you feel resentful of those around you because you start to feel unappreciated when you are compensating and sacrificing for them while doing most the work.

To avoid this, make sure your business and personal leadership vision are in writing so you can improve upon them and communicate clearly to others so they can support you.

If you are an emerging leader, meet with your leader and ask him/her to share their vision. Use your passion and talents to find ways to support their vision while still incorporating your career goals, then step up, and ask to lead those changes.

Walking your leadership talk

"Leaders are more powerful role models when they learn than when they teach." —Rosabeth Moss Kantor

The question you'll be challenged with in this section is: *Are You Walking Your Leadership Talk?*

This section is directed to those who are already leaders as well to those who are emerging leaders. If you serve in any capacity where you are responsible for others' ability to drive objectives and vision forward, or influence others to grow (including yourself), you can benefit from further development of your leadership skills.

It's been said that leaders have two basic functions: first, to meet objectives and complete the job successfully; and second, to develop and grow employees so they can complete the objectives of the job.

With so many demands, it's easy to get distracted and too focused on the first objective to get around to the second. In my work with leaders and their teams, at times, I have witnessed the loss of powerful opportunities, both for the business and individuals, primarily caused by a lack of attention to team development on the leader's part.

This lack of attention becomes a habit and quickly turns into an obstacle, preventing those leaders from accomplishing their second task of enhancing the human capacity to emerge its personal best.

Inspiring, facilitating, and developing the individuals' full potential plays a major role in contributing to the first function of leadership, "getting the job done."

In addition, having a strong team identity, which comes from individuals' strength and talents, is vital to adaptability and performing at high levels.

Recognizing the inseparability of performance and personal development is critical. Applying this knowledge in real life is challenging. We are creatures of habit and, for most of us, change is uncomfortable and can even ignite fears.

Applying the effective leadership principle of developing people requires a willingness to look deep inside, to determine what we believe for ourselves and for our organization, and to decide if we are honoring those beliefs and values in our actions.

In essence, are we "walking our leadership talk"? Are our actions aligning with our words? Are we leading change?

How are company values measured in the organization and in our relationships with individual team members?

Once we have taken the first step to create personal awareness, we can then choose to take responsibility and make necessary changes. We may need to change personal habits or develop the confidence needed to overcome obstacles that prevent us from stepping out of our comfort zone.

To be a truly effective leader one must become the change one wants to see by setting the example and acting as the "role model."

This also requires creating an environment conducive for growth and instigating a process that encourages growth, both personally and professionally. This becomes natural when you practice the first two key elements of being an empowered leader, finding your voice and inspiring change. Individuals on the team and the organization as a whole will be strengthened as you, the leader, start the growth process.

Consider beginning with these action items:

- Ask for and be open to feedback from any source and encourage support.

- Be aware that you have blind spots in your attitudes, behaviors, and actions, and be open to other perspectives.

- Monitor progress and practice celebrating success individually and with your team.

Leading is an art form, so the more you practice, the better you will be. The more you are open to role model personal growth, the faster you'll accelerate through the learning curve. Imagine having a support system that gets just as excited about the vision of the future as you do. If you could help create such a team by your own willingness to ask for help, imagine the shifts you could make in your life and those of your co-workers.

Why women make great leaders

"Some leaders are born women."

—Unknown

As we talked about earlier, women are becoming more and more willing to take risks and break the glass ceiling. Increasingly, they do not limit their place in the business world as they find their voice and value!

Women are natural leaders. We value collaboration and creating affiliations. We have inborn skills to nurture and inspire others.

I've found that women typically exhibit more strategic drive, people skills, and innovation than our male counterparts. Don't get me wrong, men have many powerful skills that come more naturally to them, some of which we could benefit from learning. Each group can learn valuable things from the other. Typically though, I find women are better at soft-power skills like listening, being democratic, and facilitating mutual agreement and benefit. Women are excellent mediators, networkers, and problem solvers. We are able to keep our cool in times of crisis and possess a willingness to develop ourselves in the face of difficulty. Certainly, some individuals are able to apply these skills and qualities more than others. Yet, we have an ability to acquire these and put them to good use when we set our mind to it. We are determined individuals when we find our purpose.

These qualities are called for to address the leadership challenges we currently face and for that reason, women have a responsibility to step up to take leadership roles and act as a role model. It is exciting and fascinating that today many women are finally doing just that! Will you be one of them?

In order to do this, you have to be willing to regularly self assess and rediscover yourself and then, for the greater good, share your lessons. This is based on my personal and professional experience in applying these principles. This is also why self-awareness is integrated into all of my programs, including my leadership program the Missing Essentials Training™.

It's my personal goal and passion to inspire women to tap into their empowered leadership skills so they can share their gifts with those they lead and powerfully impact their own lives. And why not? We are positioned to be great leaders.

Learning to lead the vision of others and walking your leadership talk will take time and patience, but with practice and determination, you will unleash unlimited opportunities for yourself and your personal support system. Imagine the possibilities!

Tying all three elements together with a client story:

I once had a consulting contract with a large corporation. As with many of my business accounts, upon assessment, I discovered there were basic infrastructure, processes, systems, and leadership skills missing that were holding the company and its employees back. I brought in one of my programs and taught about 18 individuals, a mix of supervisors, managers, and executive team members. Many of them started to make great discoveries and grow, but I recall one woman in particular, Linda, who was the most challenging and the most rewarding to work with. I tell this story because if you have ever worked in a corporation where you are not encouraged or shown how to lead, you soon lose your voice and lose sight of your value, making it difficult to stay motivated and see beyond your current situation. In fact, Linda, who was in her late fifties and had been with the company for many years, found it nearly impossible to see her way forward.

After many weeks, I was given the opportunity to work with her one on one. I was excited to finally get my hands dirty and dig through her department challenges, as I just knew together we could make changes to relieve her misery.

However, I soon found my enthusiasm wasn't being received as I had anticipated. Linda would meet with me and bring just enough to the meetings so we could keep inching along. She would come prepared with long excuses why some suggestion couldn't possibly work for her department or with her team. She would act like she was happy to work with me to my face, but when I wasn't around, she would tell others her true feelings: she wished me and all my great ideas would go away so she could go back to how things were always done. The way she was leading wasn't working for her, but it was comfortable, so she didn't want to expend the time or energy to fix it. However, judging by the little comments she leaked out, I got the impression that she secretly hoped I'd stick it out and save her from the self-defeating situation she had created.

I knew this wouldn't be easy, but I knew there was much to gain, so I stuck it out. After assessments and team meetings and being a back-seat manager to champion her along, I kept wondering when she would do what she said she wanted — lead. Finally, one day Linda and I had a bonding moment that would forever change her leadership style and lack of personal success. In one of our meetings, I carefully and assertively took Linda down a self-awareness path where, at first, she didn't want to go. With tears of relief to finally admit it, we uncovered a pearl.

Linda had been promoted into her position without additional management training. Various leaders didn't give her the mentoring and follow through she needed but still kept requiring her to perform and get better results. She did her best to draw on her skills and, for the most part, everyone liked her, especially her team. They protected Linda and saw me as the devil trying to change their leader. Why? Because Linda spent late nights, weekends, and vacation time compensating for her team's lack of performance. She felt guilty and would let them go home, but she would put in impossible hours and always be behind on her own work. Team meetings were a fun chat session, as no tasks or actions were being assigned and no follow through required. Daily schedules and responsibilities were unheard of and team members declared it couldn't be done. I could go on, but you get the picture. Why was she tolerating this situation?

Because Linda had strong limiting beliefs working against her. She was holding back her assertiveness and lacked selfconfidence and self-respect and, as a result, she couldn't expect support from her team to grow and help take on the responsibilities in their department. She was not aligned with her voice and value. Rather, she thought because she saw what needed to be done and desired it, her team would naturally see it, want it, and just do it. She didn't see that she needed to clearly voice it or inspire action and changes, and lead the change and support follow through and accountability which would bring successes and transformations for her team. She was disappointed they didn't "get it," and held to the belief they weren't capable of it because in her mind she had communicated her needs to them.

But Linda hadn't communicated her needs, and, in fact, in her meetings, whenever she shared a request or policy change, her voice would get softer and right after she'd propose it, she'd undermine it or withdraw it. She always left taking the responsibility on herself, instead of on her team.

As I dug deeper, Linda shared that she hadn't always been this way and knew better. In fact, she told me she really wanted to be a leader and spend her time doing things in that capacity, such as training her team. She even shared past professional experiences she could draw on, such as that she had previously been a teacher and loved to teach. Why then wasn't she using those skills? I challenged her about this. Would she take her students' homework home and do it for them? Would she give them an 'A' if they didn't do the assignment? Of course, she said no. Well then, I said, why are you doing this with your team? There were plenty of good reasons why she had allowed this, and we could write a whole chapter just on that. As the coach, my charge was not to judge but to help her see her power and gifts. I also encouraged her to not stay in the past, feeling guilty or beating herself up, but I tried to inspire her to make a difference now and move forward so she could connect her true inner desire with her outer goals and actions.

It was like fireworks went off inside Linda's head. The discovery of why she was holding back her team's chance to grow and her chance to use her talents to lead had happened. Something clicked with Linda, and she tapped into her value and determined to find her voice again. Over the next month, I continued to help her find her passion to lead and inspire change, to help her take on intelligent risks, to step out of her comfort zone and make requests of her team with the expectation of follow through. I helped her realize her team had untapped potential and just needed direction and inspiration. She had to become a role model, setting an example, and inspiring changes. In order to do so, she had to make some big changes too. It was a rough few weeks as her team, who had been allowed to act like spoiled children, resisted at first.

Then graduation day came, and I recall her much altered team meeting, now an empowered team meeting, where collaboration took place, assignments were reported on, ideas were generated, and smiles and celebrations were shared. This was because the team felt inspired and a part of the overall vision. Linda took a few minutes to openly acknowledge her transformation and the challenges and defining moments along her journey. She assured the team she was there to stay and that the differences they noticed in her leadership and in the department would stay. And you know what? A team resistant to the transformation at first acknowledged her changes and appreciated her efforts because they felt not only were they better, but they saw she was better, too. And they felt it was about time.

ᏚᏣᏔᏓ

I hope this story motivates and challenges you to act as a role model and take action. Take time for self-awareness and assessment, to find and be driven by your voice, to inspire through the power of influence, and to lead change in your life and with those you are fortunate to serve!

The pitfalls of not applying the three key elements are:

- Lack of ideas and collaboration from those you lead
- Feeling isolated by a lack of support to achieve the bigger vision
- Reacting more than being proactive
- Not able to speak up or share your opinion, ideas, or values
- May feel walked over — have boundary issues
- Self confidence can be easily toppled
- Feel like you are working on someone else's vision
- You push and pull more than you guide or lead
- Time management is an issue because you are focused on too many areas or your team doesn't know how to support you

The benefits of applying the three key elements are:

- Collaboration increases
- You have the increased support and resources necessary to carry out the bigger vision
- You live an inspired and fulfilling life as you become a passionately empowered leader in your life and work
- There is increased personal drive which results in increased energy, motivation, and ability to focus
- Your leadership style changes and you are able to accelerate results
- You can easily identify roadblocks that prevent others from supporting you and the bigger vision
- You lead by example, causing others to stretch out of their comfort zones and share their gifts and talents

Wrapping up

Your self-awareness is directly linked to your ability to be an empowered leader. You have to be a leader of yourself first before you can lead others.

You must know your skills, your abilities, and innate strengths in order to lead the vision of others. This is a fundamental principle of leadership.

You must be willing to develop in the face of difficulty and view your failures or lack of success as learning opportunities that you can share to benefit others' growth. Then get up and keep going!

Honor the power of influence you have as a confident woman by allowing others to shine around you and asking and getting feedback on your performance. Be open to having a mentor or coach and learn from their feedback and perspective of you.

Be open to leading by example, to become a role-model and through your actions and words, inspire others.

You don't have to be in an official role to become an empowered leader; instead, begin with showing up and leading passionately in all areas of your life! Work to keep your voice alive! Practice getting in touch with the power and gifts you possess every day by sharing them with others.

Where to go from here?

Now that you have reviewed all the **Six Power Zone Principles**™, take time to ponder these questions:

- Where have you found your voice and value during reading and self-exploration?

- What has inspired changes in you? Where are you inspired to go from here?

- What changes have you begun to lead in your life? What changes would you like to continue or to lead next?

The process and principles you have learned are meant to be used continually in your life, and each time you revisit them work to further integrate them. For example, review your Vision of Success statement and add to it or choose another item to use to work through the principles. Challenge yourself to take risks to embrace the next part of your journey to success. Create a plan, identify your blockers, demonstrate your new confidence with the qualities, and show up as a leader in all areas of your life. Each time you do this, you will reap rewards and desire more and more to fulfill your possibilities by leading your life from your Power Zone.

ℰℭℛ

"You have enormous untapped power that you will probably never tap, because most people never run far enough on their first wind to ever find they have a second wind." —William James

Ten Steps to Your Empowerment

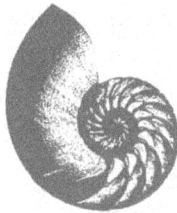

1. Pinpoint your power zone! This is where you feel excited, joyful, balanced, and peaceful. When in touch with it, you can work at the speed of light, you're creative and passionate, things come easy, and you take pleasure in your natural ability by using your talents and skills. You don't feel drained and your energy increases when you work from here. Recognize when you're moving away from or doing something not aligned with your power zone by listening to your gut. Pay attention to why are you not excited about something, feel confused, or not interested in it. Listen to your body's response. By doing so, you'll know when you have found your power zone and when you are leading your life from it!

2. Start on your journey to success! Begin with creating your Vision of Success statement then practice using the principles to draw it closer to you. Build a habit of creating regular focus on the statement before making it too big, as that can make you feel overwhelmed and quit before you try. As new habits form, add to your vision, broaden it with additional goals such as the lifestyle you wish to live, relationships you want to attract, opportunities you seek, even the income you want to make. Read it every day and compare your attitude, intentions, and actions to it.

3. Stop tolerating and push though the garbage in your head! Let go of the need to be right or the fear of what others may think. Face your unhealthy and limiting thinking and behaviors once and for all. Then determine to take the intelligent risks and bold steps necessary to leave your comfort zone so you can start living your Vision of Success.

4. Don't shoot yourself in the foot! Know where you stand by creating a Focus Action Plan and then use it and adjust it as needed. When you complete one, create another one. Notice when you get out of the habit of following and come back to what works. This will make prioritizing and determining what you can handle on your plate easier. Use this plan for your business goals too. Don't forget to celebrate your successes.

5. Don't take on the Four Confidence Blockers by sheer willpower! Use the CRES System to do a selfassessment and create commitments of how you'll shift your energy and overcome them. Changing just one will create a positive chain reaction. Notice when you handle a situation differently than you might have previously done. This is not a little thing; it signifies using your power of choice to change. Reward yourself for doing so!

6. Throw away your scorecard! As women, we have a tendency to make up our own scorecard from negative expectations for ourselves and how we think others perceive us. Subconsciously, we work to meet these unfavorable expectations. Realize that others don't hold as much importance on your scorecard as you do. You are free to change and others will adapt. If your expectations of yourself are not working, throw them out and create new ones. Only look back to avoid repeating or to celebrate your new score.

7. Get out of the passenger seat and into the driver's seat of your life! Quit being the great task-doer and instead create the legacy you want to leave behind. Setting your day up for success is a vital step to achieve this. Determine what your daily measurement of success is. Ask yourself what a successful day would look like to you and how it would feel. Then compare your tasks, actions, and attitude to see where you need to adjust. Set clear expectations of yourself and others. Then take responsibility and follow through.

8. Change your thinking, change your energy, change your results! It's so important to take advantage of this universal law. You can't have sustainable energy to see your vision through without this. Your personal energy comes from how you feel about yourself and the choices you make, which dictate your success. While one negative thought can take you off track, change your focus, and lower your energy, one mental shift can positively modify your immediate situation and improve your life in other areas you didn't realize were affected by it.

9. Dispel the myth and mask! It is not an unforgivable offense to not have all the answers and ask for help when you need it. Check to make sure you're using your newfound confidence gracefully. Be open to regular selfassessment and feedback from others so the qualities of a confident woman will work for you. Look for evidence of the mask of confidence in your own life and notice others' masks to teach them how to remove it.

10. Embrace your greatness! Whether as a mother, care taker, co-worker, executive or business leader, you must embrace your personal greatness. Identify your own seashell and what you have or will do with it. Use your unique voice to make a difference in your own   and others' lives. Don't take the power of influence you have as a woman for granted. Use your natural ability to inspire others to dream and achieve bigger dreams! Boldly go to the edge in what you believe in. Lead changes in your life. Keep targeting your vision and your legacy will take form. Show up, be present, and notice others who need to find their greatness and help them lead their lives from the power zone.

Final Thoughts

I have always been determined, and as a general rule, when I put my mind to it, I can make most things happen. I was the one in six kids who, when given a challenge the others wouldn't dare, would say, "Watch me." I went to junior college and high school at the same time. After graduation at age 20, I became a dental assistant instructor. A few short years later, I took a break and joined my ex-husband on the road. We traveled the country from behind the wheel of a 50foot semi truck. Yes, I drove those big, beastly trucks. I had a passion for horses, but riding wasn't enough, I was part of a drill team that won the western state championship two years in a row. When leaving my abusive marriage, I fired my attorney, and through self-taught knowledge, I did what my former attorney claimed was impossible: against my exhusband's attorney, I successfully obtained a permanent order to protect my children from the past situation. And as I walked out of the courtroom, a man ran up to me asking which law firm I was with in order to offer me a job at his firm. I smiled as I told him I wasn't an attorney, but it sure felt good to be mistaken for one. It's amazing what a mama bear can do!

I'm sure you get my point — I have the gift to look beyond the status quo, to stretch the boundaries of my comfort zone, and see other possibilities, which is my overarching goal for you. Some come out of necessity, some with more grace than others, and some as more enjoyable experiences than others.

Understanding this about myself, I feel I've been destined to go after more all my life. I still feel I have more to achieve and a larger journey ahead. Growth is natural, and I am a cardcarrying student of life. Keep in mind, there have been periods when I forgot how to use my personal greatness, and I let my voice go silent. When I became reacquainted with my gifts and talents so my driving core energy started to flow through me again, I saw the brilliance of my power zone once again, and I haven't let go since. It is so important for you to learn how to recognize, claim, and use your power zone to influence your life.

From my power zone, ego and fear don't hold me back. I filter life differently through my vision of success. I have enough courage to push past my protective shell to find a higher self-trust and increased energy. I don't run from success; I embrace it. As I have paid attention and fine-tuned my ability to stay in touch, I have been able to let go of past hang ups and restricting beliefs. I quit trying to prove what no longer works for me, instead focusing on what inspires me and allows me to make a difference by helping others to also stay in touch with their power zones.

It is so liberating to lead your life from your power zone! You let go of what doesn't work — including appointments, projects, and poor boundaries that don't honor yourself. You won't feel the draining energy from things you "should" or "have" to do. By showing up 100 percent in life and work, the internal conflict and turmoil evaporate. You work from your values, and it is easier to make decisions that work for you. You can see opportunities outside yourself that will help you to grow bigger dreams for yourself. You can show up and play bigger!

Leading my life from my power zone helps me feel a stronger connection to my life, and I allow more of the right things into my life. I look at taking risks with wonder and possibility. I no longer measure my time by how busy I am but rather if I am focused on the right things, ones that honor my vision and allow me to work from my powerful self, and I feel happy and successful.

Although I want you to feel my passion for what I believe in, please know I can relate to you. I live in the real world, with a business to run, relationships to nurture, everyday responsibilities, challenges to overcome, a special needs teenager to support through her life journey, extended family dynamics, a loving husband with his own dreams, and so on. All of this is life. My point is that you'll have ebb and flow in your life, adversities will happen, with joys and successes in between them. I firmly believe, amidst the rhythm of life, you can stay tapped into your true self and not lose yourself to circumstances and challenges but find and cultivate your personal greatness.

Don't put off your happiness and success until a so-called perfect time. Run out and make it perfect for you.

Don't give away your personal power! It's a myth that it goes away or someone can take it away. That's not possible, but I see women give away their power all the time. Most commonly, women do this through their words. We tell people how to treat us as less than we are. We tell ourselves we are not deserving of more. Women need to reach a place where they say nothing about themselves that doesn't reflect what they want to do, be, or become. I feel strongly that what holds women back is their own self doubt. And when a woman recognizes her suppressing thoughts and behaviors and takes proactive steps to change, she will feel fulfilled, and her life will begin to change. She'll be happier, healthier, and more productive. She'll use her natural gifts, talents, and skills to release her creativity and inspiration. She will have a whole new sense of who she is.

What can you do, be, or become by leading your life from the power zone?

Only you can answer this question. I have witnessed amazing transformations when my clients apply the Six Power Zone

Principles™ in their life. I've seen it take their personal and professional lives in a whole new direction. I've seen it heal old wounds, bring about personal forgiveness, and squelch the internal battle of what one is deserving or worthy of.

Leaving your comfort zone means taking some big steps. First, you've got to be very clear about what's most important to you. This enables you to create a Vision of Success, a blueprint you can carry forward as you reapply this system again and again.

You may need to exercise patience and trust that you are on the right path. You may even need to have a courageous conversation to ask for support. Your energy will be infectious to some and intimidating to others.

One special note about your loved ones, friends and colleagues— as they witness you growing, changing, and blossoming into a confident woman, they may validate these changes or they may push against them. It's possible they may not even be aware they're doing this.

Stay aware of when you're using your best qualities by honoring the power that comes with being a confident woman. And don't let others' fears of leaving their comfort zone hold you back from leaving yours and stepping into your greatness.

Seek to spend more time with those who are supportive of the changes you're trying to make, especially women who have the confident qualities that you're working towards.

While this process is powerful when applied, it is meant to integrate with your knowledge and skills. Adapt it for your life. If something doesn't work for you, don't do it. My goal here is to help you see beyond your current comfort zone and challenge you to go to the next level in your life. You define what that means to you.

I hope you are getting excited to put this to the test. I hope you've found your purpose, the one you came in search of at the start of our journey. I trust that you are already well on your way to leading your life from the power zone.

As you apply this process, be patient with yourself. Practice allowing yourself to notice even the smallest changes in your transformation. Believe in yourself and in your capabilities, and let go of what you can't control. Enjoy your journey to success.

Remember, it's a lifelong journey so celebrate your successes along the way. Help others with their journey. Be bold and brave as you leave your comfort zone. Get comfortable with the thrill of excitement and even the panic. Then make the leap of heart and mind to embrace the new powerful you!

To your journey to success,

René Johnson

The Power Zone Coach

About the Author

René Johnson is passionate about helping women lead their lives from their power zones. Her personal story is one of courage and defining moments, which led to her life path of coaching. René is a certified empowerment coach and a graduate of the Institute for Professional Excellence in Coaching (iPEC), an institute accredited by the International Coach Federation (ICF). She launched Emerggy Coaching, LLC in 2004 and Power Zone Coaching, LLC in 2009. She believes that behind every successful woman is her most powerful self, and that when women tap into their power zones they can overcome any fears or doubts they may face.

René's mission is to support women in every area, whether in their personal and professional lives or in their businesses, so that they may find their full voice and value and be inspired to direct change in their own lives and then powerfully influence those they lead. She has authored several business continuing education international courses, published articles and ebooks, as well as developed the Power Zone Mastery™ and Missing Essentials Training™ programs. In addition to working with individual clients and professional organizations across the country, René is a sought-after motivational speaker who has appeared before audiences of lawmakers, educators, and business leaders.

Wherever possible, René shares her talents, skills and passions by volunteering in community associations and speaking at events which support women.

René has two daughters, five adorable grandchildren.

Website: powerzonecoach.com

POWER ZONE
Mastery™

Reader Bonus

Readers of this book will receive a 10% savings on the
Power Zone Mastery™ program. The author, René Johnson,
will lead you through a journey of self discovery, revealing
the hidden pearls within you. By using the strategies
contained in this book, along with additional tools and
resources, you will be able to catapult yourself to a higher
level of success and happiness. René is excited to see you
apply these powerful methods and not just read about them!

To register for the next tele-class, go to:
www.powerzonemastery.com
Use coupon code (LYCZREADER)

Whether you read this book in a library, your office or
someone gave it to you, it doesn't matter. Anyone can
participate!

For keynote presentations and additional resources
Please visit
René Johnson at

powerzonecoach.com